Diplomacy and Disillusion at the Court
of Margaret Thatcher

BY THE SAME AUTHOR

End of Empire: The Demise of the Soviet Union, Washington, DC, 1993.

Can the Soviet System Survive Reform? Seven Colloquies about the State of Soviet Socialism Seven Decades after the Bolshevik Revolution, London and New York, 1989.

Stalinism: Its Impact on Russia and the World, London and New York, 1982.

Communist Reformation: Nationalism, Internationalism and Change in the World Communist Movement, London, 1979.

Eurocommunism: Its Roots and Future in Italy and Elsewhere, London, 1978.

Hazards of Learning: An International Symposium on the Crisis of the University, La Salle, IL, 1977.

Détente, London, 1976.

Toynbee on Toynbee: A Conversation Between Arnold J. Toynbee and G. R. Urban, New York, 1974.

DIPLOMACY
and DISILLUSION
at THE COURT *of*
Margaret THATCHER

AN INSIDER'S VIEW

GEORGE R. URBAN

I.B. Tauris Publishers

LONDON · NEW YORK

Published in 1996 by I.B.Tauris & Co Ltd
Victoria House, Bloomsbury Square, London WC1B 4DZ

175 Fifth Avenue, New York NY 10010

In the United States of America and in Canada
distributed by St Martin's Press
175 Fifth Avenue, New York NY 10010

A full CIP record for this book is available from the British
Library

A full CIP record for this book is available from the Library of
Congress

ISBN 1 86064 084 2

Library of Congress catalog card number available

Set in Monotype Ehrhardt by Ewan Smith, London

Printed and bound in Great Britain by
WBC Ltd, Bridgend, Mid Glamorgan

Contents

Acknowledgements

I have tried to report in this volume, with whatever accuracy I was able to muster, the facts and ideas I encountered in the course of my contacts with Baroness Thatcher both as prime minister and out of office. Yet I am aware that there is a bias built into the work of every diarist: his own role and thinking tend to occupy a more prominent place in his story than they would or did in the eyes of disinterested observers. The notes here published may well suffer from that deficiency. If so, I am confident that friends and colleagues who witnessed what I did will liberally provide their correctives.

I owe a profound debt of gratitude to Lord Thomas of Swynnerton, without whose friendship and encouragement I would not have been in a position to serve and then to criticize the policies of Margaret Thatcher.

My debt to Charles Douglas-Home is of a less definable kind but no less profound. His untimely death in 1985 deprived British public life of an irreplaceable moral influence and his friends of a mentor and an inspiration.

I am especially grateful to Patricia Urban, who played midwife to the birth of this volume and promoted its growth at all its stages.

Diplomacy and Disillusion at the Court
of Margaret Thatcher

Introduction

The diary entries in this volume draw on recordings I made for my personal oral history collection between 1981 and 1994. In deciding to publish them I had to balance the rival claims of confidentiality and history. For many years, the ethics of personal trust militated against disclosure. It would certainly have been inappropriate to make my notes public while Margaret Thatcher was in office. Allowing the Soviet side to take the measure of Western thinking in high places would have run counter to everything I stood for.

But with the ebb and flow of the Thatcher era receding into the background and the Cold War safely (as it seems) behind us, I am persuaded that imparting my impressions of Margaret Thatcher 'at work and thought' should be no longer delayed. The highways and byways of the mental processes of our elected rulers are of manifest concern to those who elect them. After a decent lapse of time, they are or should be public property.

Timely disclosure is especially pertinent to our understanding of Margaret Thatcher's long and famous service as prime minister. Her administrations were the most radical and her personal impact on government and public opinion the most idiosyncratic since the first British Labour government after the war. For good or for evil, she impinged on every aspect of British self-understanding and on the understanding of the British abroad. Her eleven years in office saw the most dramatic shift in the world balance of power since 1918. To comprehend the reactions of the British mind to those eventful years one has to comprehend first the mind of Margaret Thatcher.

Other factors, too, militated for publication at the right time. I felt I had to depict the curve of my own attitudes to Margaret

Thatcher, beginning with my enthusiastic support of her 'cleanse-the-Augean-stables' kind of policies at home and her sharp critique of the Soviet system in foreign affairs, and ending with my profound disagreement with her attacks on the European Community. My exasperation, after her fall, at seeing her wrapped in ideological rectitude of a rather obsessional kind was only partly stilled by her fighting stand on Bosnia, which I shared and tried to carry forward.

Also, in her memoirs[1], with one exception, Margaret Thatcher avoids mentioning the extramural assistance she often invited from and was liberally given by academic supporters. The names of Lord Thomas, Sir Michael Howard, Leonard Schapiro, Hugh Seton-Watson, Brian Crozier, Gordon Craig, Fritz Stern, Norman Stone, Timothy Garton Ash – to mention but a few – are conspicuous by their absence. Here, too, the gaps had to be filled in if only to remove pitfalls from the paths of future historians. Finally, the misrepresentation in the British press of how Margaret Thatcher was advised on Germany at her 1990 Chequers seminar has caused me, and I believe some of the other participants, considerable pain. Far from harbouring anti-German sentiments, I am an admirer of the achievements of the German Federal Republic and an advocate of vastly improved Anglo-German relations under the European Union. So, I believe, were most of the other Chequers advisers. To have shown us in a contrary light was a travesty. Here, too, I have attempted to put the record straight by publishing my diary notes in full.

Going beyond these specific factors, I felt it to be in the public interest to bring close to the reader a mind both painstakingly precise and passionate. With her qualifications in chemistry and law, Margaret Thatcher bestrode a wide area of the human experience, and even where her sympathies were less than even-handed, she was always keen to hear the opposite side of a favoured argument. Those not involved in the hectic pursuit of politics and unfamiliar with the vanity of politicians may not readily appreciate just how distressing

1. Margaret Thatcher, *The Downing Street Years*, London, 1993.

that can be. In less enlightened times, shooting the messenger was the vizier's answer to the purveyor of such tidings. Rumours to the contrary notwithstanding, in matters of the intellect Margaret Thatcher has been a model of broadminded tolerance.

As an occasional adviser on the Cold War and communist affairs, I saw more of the passionate side of Margaret Thatcher than that of cool reason, and I found this at times both revealing and agreeable, for in my conception, too, our ideological contest with the Soviet system and Soviet power was about moral values, or it was about nothing. Moral outrage was, as it had to be, the mainspring of our opposition to totalitarianism. From that, and not from any power-calculus alone, followed all the practical policies Margaret Thatcher's administrations put in train in the international domain between 1979 and 1990. I rejoiced in this primacy of moral concepts and did my best to reinforce Margaret Thatcher's identification with them. 'Right' and 'wrong' became useable words again in public discourse – a welcome change after the grey and ineffectual relativism and utilitarianism of earlier British governments and the psycho-babble of the chattering classes.

Whether Margaret Thatcher's passions were always harnessed to causes most deserving of them is another matter. The reader will find my own views clearly stated: her evocation, in her final years in power, of the ghosts of nationalism and chauvinism, and her provocative attacks on European integration and its leaders, were unworthy of the great spirit that animated her policies in so many other areas, and indeed of her earlier views as a supporter of European integration. They alienated much of the Continent and may prove extremely damaging for the future peace of Europe. Nationalism, once aroused, can be played by many hands and to devastating effect. Of course, in the real world, some form of balance-of-power politics may, alas, be unavoidable. But to promote it from high office and make it respectable again is to insult the memory of those millions of young Europeans who perished over the centuries in our fratricidal wars in the name of preserving the balance of power. Surely, more imaginative counsels are called for. Nowhere did late Thatcherism

3

fail the British people more thoroughly than in its failure to recognize that the locus of such imaginative counsels can only be a generously supported programme of European integration.

Another area where I found Margaret Thatcher's passions working for a diminishing asset was her long identification with Mikhail Gorbachev. I shared her respect for this untypical and personable Soviet leader. But Margaret Thatcher, having, as she thought, 'discovered' Gorbachev, developed a sense of proprietary rights over him. This was misjudged and a little arrogant. Her kinship with the Soviet leader has often been ascribed to a shared chemistry; if so, it was a chemistry in which the emotional ingredient predominated over all others. Gorbachev's immense contribution to the West's triumph in the Cold War is beyond dispute, even though he liked it to be understood that the Kremlin, too, had won the Cold War – by losing it. Without him the Soviet system and empire may not have collapsed as rapidly or as peacefully as they did. Whether Gorbachev's intention was limited to making the Soviet Union fit for an improved form of communism and nothing else, is hardly germane to the outcome. The system was beyond repair, and the attempt to reform it ended in foreseeable disaster.

Yet such was Margaret Thatcher's faith in Gorbachev that she was slow to recognize his vanishing support and his limitations as an engine of reform. And by hesitating to detach herself from him in time (and confirming the Americans in their own hesitancy) she fuelled an impression in many West European minds that the British prime minister was not only supporting to the last the failing Soviet leader for reasons obscure to the eyes of the uninitiated, but was also keen to preserve a strong – albeit liberalized and market-based – Soviet state as a force of world stability. All this alienated Ukraine, too, as well as some of the other independence-seeking Soviet republics, which had their own bitter experience of what stability and normalization could mean under Soviet auspices.

Among Britain's allies in Europe the Thatcherite indulgence of Gorbachev was encouraging a view that, no sooner had the Soviet enemy begun to falter, than Albion, now pushed politically, too, to the edge of Europe, was back at its perfidious game, looking for fresh alliances to promote narrow national interests. The plan, to the extent that it seriously existed, was a non-starter. Neither France nor Russia would oblige, but that it should have been at all contemplated was a sign of Margaret Thatcher's limited understanding of how the tectonic changes in the East could be made to benefit the whole of Europe and, indeed, the whole of Western civilization.

The roots of these misjudgements were many. Emotional factors apart, neither she nor Whitehall as a whole had a comprehensive understanding of Eastern and Central Europe at the social, cultural and historical levels. Academic input, while greatly assisting the prime minister, was cordially resented by government departments. Nor, in many cases, was reality allowed to interfere with certain dated and prejudicial views of what Germany and France were about under contemporary conditions. The past, and especially the symbolism of the Second World War and the empire, still loomed large in Margaret Thatcher's imagination; the present, with Britain attempting to punch above its weight, seemed unmanageable; and the future in the East called for a master-plan which neither Britain nor any other country was able or willing to design, much less to finance.

A 'Forty-Five-Years' War' had ended, and the world found itself in the throes of what amounted to typically postwar upheavals; but our leaders were unprepared. The very magnitude of the tasks ahead paralysed them. Their chancelleries were bulging with war scenarios, but they had no plans for the peaceful exit of the Soviet system and empire. The Gulf War and the collapse of Yugoslavia added to their disorientation. A Marshall Plan of sorts was briefly contemplated, but that, too, became the victim of the general cluelessness. Economic recession increased the pain of any decision-making. None of the better minds in the public domain was gripped by a passionate longing to impose order on the debris of the fallen dictatorships.

The penalty for all these failures of the Western will and imagination was not long in coming. Within six years of the expiry of the communist system, Roman Catholic Lithuania, then Roman Catholic Poland with its famous record of having undermined the entire rationale of Soviet-style communism, and then Hungary with its proud legacy of the 1956 revolution, returned, in free elections, ex-communist or fellow-travelling parliamentary or presidential majorities, or indeed both. Some of the other countries followed suit. Russia, Ukraine and Romania had never changed personnel. The symbolism of the fall of President Lech Wałęsa[1] in November 1995 to the former Communist Party functionary and junior minister, Aleksandr Kwaśniewski, was especially poignant. Nikita Khrushchev would have enjoyed the spectacle. He did not manage to 'bury' us,[2] but neither did we do what we ought to have done to eradicate the heritage of Sovietism. Here was proof of the most telling kind of the ineptitude of Western statesmanship. Seldom has victory been so cheaply bought or so mindlessly squandered.

It may, indeed, well have been the 'cheapness' of victory that prevented our leaders and Western public opinion from seeing what precisely was at stake. Had American servicemen perished in their thousands on the North German plain, and had Washington been reduced to ashes in the pursuit of a comparable Western victory, I am inclined to believe that America would have rushed to the generous rehabilitation of Eastern and Central Europe and probably of Russia as well. But as no high drama materialized, no funds materialized either to still the frustrations of the freshly liberated. Even so modest a proposal as the reduction of some of the external tariffs of the European Union *vis-à-vis* Eastern Europe overtaxed the political will of the West European leaders.

It would be inaccurate and unjust to imply that Margaret Thatcher was responsible for these calamities. For one thing, she was prime minister of a medium-sized power, perhaps with a piece of influence in Washington greater than Britain's economic strength warranted, but nevertheless only one of several and not the most

---

1. Leader, under communism, of the rebellious trades union movement 'Solidarity'; Polish president 1990–95. Defeated in the November 1995 presidential election by Aleksandr Kwaśniewski, a former communist minister.
2. 'History is on our side. We will bury you.' N. S. Khrushchev at the Polish Embassy in Moscow, November 1956 (*The Times*, 19 November 1956).

important. Both Germany and France figured larger in the American calculations, and this for the commonsensical reason that France was central to the construction of a united Europe, which Britain was not, and Germany, especially a reunited Germany, central to the rehabilitation of Eastern and Central Europe, which Britain was not. Britain could have been central to one or the other, or both, had the British people been less given to illusions after victory in 1945 and better served by their leaders; but they were not. 'It is the penalty of greatness', Bryce wrote about the final stage of the Holy Roman Empire, 'that its form should outlive its substance: that gilding and trappings should remain when that which they were meant to deck and clothe has departed.'[1] Germany was now in a different league from both France and Britain, and President Clinton and his team lost no time in recognizing Germany's primacy. Hence any good or damage Britain could have done in Eastern and Central Europe, with or without Margaret Thatcher, was limited.

The time factor, too, exonerates Margaret Thatcher from most of the blame. She lost power in the early stages of the post-communist denouement, in November 1990. From then on, her voice, while still powerful as rhetoric, was heard from the sidelines and carried only moral authority. For a surprisingly long time, however, her charisma outside Britain remained unimpaired. This was especially so in the United States, where she acquired the status of a household celebrity, and in Russia and the other former communist lands, where her special combination of femininity and tough talk, as well as her long commitment to Eastern European freedom and independence, intrigued and attracted the most diverse audiences of both genders. But gratifying as her popularity abroad must have appeared to her at the time, it was an epilogue. Her less than modest call to arms, on 9 March 1996, in the spirit, as she claimed, of Winston Churchill's 'Iron Curtain' speech at Fulton, Missouri, was an exercise in nostalgia, no more.

After her ill-conceived attempt to prevent or delay the unification

---

1. *The Holy Roman Empire*, London, 1941 edition, p. 401.

of Germany had failed, Margaret Thatcher's residual influence on shaping the reconstruction of Eastern and Central Europe and the deconstruction of the legacy of communist rule shrank quickly. She was still in a position to warn, encourage, discourage and remonstrate, and she did so on many occasions and in many places, but her influence no longer reached beyond the spoken word. The retrograde results of the 1992–95 elections cannot, therefore, be laid at her doorstep.

True, her reluctance to countenance the rescue of state-owned lame-duck industries, on which the vast majority of employment in the East depended, and her enthusiasm for privatization, were in conflict with her overall ambition to make liberal democracy and the free market widely acceptable to the population; in the end, dogma prevailed over pragmatism. But it is no less true that the radical, shock-therapy type of reforms were not her policy alone. In some countries, moreover – notably in the Czech Republic and Poland – they appeared to work, even though they were deeply unpopular.

We have to be clear that by the end of 1989, 'Thatcherism' of sorts was the West's (as well as the East's) agreed economic formula for the whole of Eastern and Central Europe, Russia included. There was a consensus that parliamentary democracy, the drastic reduction of the state sector, privatization and the re-establishment of the rules of the market had to be introduced as a single package. Only the speed and scope of the reforms were subject to debate. Speed and scope, however, proved critical to the outcome. How were these to be gauged? Not for the first time in East–West relations, we had been poorly served by our economists, for no one in the West had foreseen just how thoroughly the command economies had rendered the whole of Eastern and Central Europe unfit for the resumption of normal economic activity. The decline was deep and extensive, affecting the people's minds as much as infrastructure, production and resources. Civil society had been destroyed. Public morale, already low in the wake of communist rule, was plumbing new depths.

It is clear enough in retrospect – it should have been clear at the time – that, in the absence of any master plan for the rehabilitation

8

of the area, Western calls for a speedy economic transformation should either not have been made, or made only with qualifications. But as no master-plan was forthcoming and assistance of an all-encompassing kind was limited to the special case of East Germany, and that through the exertions of West Germany, the Eastern belief in Western goodwill and capitalist omniscience disintegrated as sharply as it had arisen. With it, 'Thatcherism', too, though not its author, fell from grace; suddenly, the ideas of Margaret Thatcher, as applied by local palaeo-capitalists and mafiosi, became the whipping-boys for much that had gone wrong since 1989.

Western investors, too, were increasingly seen as predators. Their sole concern was said to be unscrupulous enrichment – never mind the reconstruction of Eastern Europe. Such charges, we must concede in fairness, were not without an element of truth. Acquiring national assets at nominal rates or creating monopolistic controls in the media were, indeed, temptations few Western investors could resist; and Britain was in a poor position to object, seeing that 60 per cent of the more serious British press was in the hands of two non-resident foreigners – both standard-bearers of the Thatcherite corpus of ideas.

Up and down most of these formerly anti-communist lands, communist predictions about the rapacious nature of capitalism were now gleefully quoted. The resentment was civilized but severe. By 1995, the joke was more on the hubris of the West than on communism: the communist origins of the bankruptcy of 1989 were conveniently ignored. How Hegel would have loved this roguish display of the 'cunning of history'.

Less tangible factors, too, played important roles. Our insistence on speed and a seamless capitalism was conceived in a historical, social and cultural vacuum. In Russia, the economic defeat of the Soviet Union was felt to be a Russian national, more than a Soviet, humiliation. This was bound to rankle. In Hungary, Poland, Czechoslovakia and the Baltic states, however, 'defeat' was experienced as so many victories over both communism and Russian hegemony. The Russian collapse was self-inflicted; the misery of

Central Europe was not. The first had its origins in Lenin, the second in Yalta.

There arose also a problem of language. The popular Western inclination to lump the Soviet Union and its client states cavalierly together as 'communist nations' and 'communist economies' closed many Eastern European minds – minds which had been wide open to the West in 1989. Semantic carelessness gave great offence. Words and notions inaccurately used were judged to be giveaway symbols of Western ignorance and indifference. And so they were. The Clinton administration's 'Russia-first'-ism added force to the impression that the West was more concerned with rehabilitating the old oppressor than the victims of oppression. Rational or otherwise, the policy alienated the West's natural allies without manifestly reforming or appeasing a still powerful Russian empire.

The West's advocacy of speed, moreover, took no account of the rudimentary but none the less real social and economic security which the man and woman in the street had come to take for granted under 'socialism'. Worse, it failed to anticipate their likely reaction to the loss of social security under democracy and the free market. Social dislocation and the pauperization of a large part of the population (greatly in excess of communist poverty levels) were uninviting introductions to Westernization, 'Europe' and capitalism. The massive benefits the West had said over the decades would come the citizens' way once they had shed the shackles of the totalitarian system failed to materialize, certainly in the short or medium term. Cultural pessimism, always widespread in the former Habsburg lands, made the pain of transition seem even worse than the figures warranted. Anomie predominated; the 'feel-bad' factor was universal. In 1992–93, about 70 per cent of White Russians, Ukrainians and Hungarians nursed a 'positive' view of the same communist system they had repudiated with such vigour only three years earlier. In 1994 real wages, as a percentage of real wages in 1989, were: 88.30 in Hungary; 62.40 in Bulgaria; 32.80 in Lithuania, and 63.80 in Russia. Unsurprisingly, in the December 1995 Russian Parliamentary elections, the communists, with 22 per cent of the vote, established themselves as the strongest party, winning, with their Agrarian Party ally, a third of the seats in the Duma. The ire of Russia's 30 million inflation-wracked pensioners and millions of unpaid workers had struck home. In March 1996 the Duma voted overwhelmingly for the re-creation of the Soviet Union.

But a balance must be drawn. My concern here is not the Cold War as such or its aftermath, but Margaret Thatcher's part in them to the extent I was able to assist her and observe her. It could never be expected that the Thatcher type of economic radicalism, with its focus entirely on the collectivistic excesses of overgrown but democratic Western welfare states, could be rapidly applied to countries attempting to make the unprecedented transition from totalitarian regimentation and a command economy to parliamentary democracy and the free market – under Eastern and Central European cultural conditions to boot.

Russia, with its long tradition of collectivism and inexperience of democracy, stood out as providing a contrast *par excellence* and the most formidable (and arguably unanswerable) challenge; but even Poland, Hungary, Czechoslovakia, Romania, Bulgaria and the Baltic states were in various degrees ill-suited to or unready for fundamental remedies. Even where the private sector began to make spectacular progress (as in the Czech Republic), egalitarianism, full employment, the state provision of generous welfare benefits, and various safety nets on the German and Scandinavian patterns continued to be articles of faith with which the rules of the market were not to be allowed to interfere. In any case, the organization of the economy was only one factor making these countries substantially different from Western Europe; culture was another and the more important. Not to have recognized all this was an error; not to have thrown a lifeline to the East in the form of Marshall Plan-type assistance was culpable. Here was an opportunity to make intelligent use of any 'peace dividend' accruing from a war we had won but, mercifully, did not have to shed blood for. It was left unexploited.

In the last analysis, Margaret Thatcher's reputation as one of the principal architects of Western victory in the Cold War is only marginally affected by the fortunes of 'Thatcherism' in Eastern and Central Europe. For many years, and with iron consistency, she hammered away at the evils of totalitarianism and lived to see it collapse. That, and her galvanization of the British people at a time of accelerating decline, temporary though that galvanization may turn out to be, is what history will mainly remember.

Margaret Thatcher's entitlement to be counted among the significant in the British pantheon would be unchallengeable had she not jeopardized it by a narrow and shortsighted conception of Britain's place in Europe and Europe's place in the minds of the British people. The good she has done on the domestic scene may or may not prove lasting, but the sound of the damage done to Britain's bonds with its friends and partners on the Continent, and thus to the British national interest, is certain to go on resonating in the consciousness of Europe. I saw Margaret Thatcher both in her mode of greatness and in her unedifying moods of off-shore nationalism. My notes in this volume trace her path from one to the other.

NOTES FROM MY DIARY

CHAPTER I

Preparing for Reagan

It looks simple enough in retrospect: the triumphant march of the Soviet system and empire in the 1970s ground to a halt in the early 1980s and ended in the collapse of both under the weight of their inherent absurdities.

At the time, however, it was far from certain that such would be the course of history. The 1980–81 crisis of communism in Poland need not have spilt over, in 1985–89, to the rest of Eastern/Central Europe and the Soviet Union itself had the Soviet leadership under Leonid Brezhnev decided to invade Poland and eradicate dissent, as the East German leader Erich Honecker[1] and the Bulgarian president Todor Zhivkov[2] were fervently advocating. The Soviet intervention in Afghanistan could have been pressed home with greater vigour and brought to an acceptable conclusion before Soviet casualties mounted. Andropov might have survived, economic reform succeeded; and, certainly in early 1981, there was no foretelling that the prime ministership of Margaret Thatcher, and more significantly the 'Reagan factor', would so powerfully accelerate the fall of Soviet communism.

Indeed, the question on all Western lips at the time was about the collapse not of the Soviet system, but of our own. Jean-François Revel's *How Democracies Perish*[3] caught the mood of the period to perfection. Liberal democracy was widely thought to be doomed – Marxism of sorts and the advance of Soviet influence the wave of the future.

That Margaret Thatcher sought unconventional advice to underpin her instinctive reactions to the march of the Soviet system need not surprise us under the circumstances. Her forte had always been domestic

---

1. Head of state of the German Democratic Republic, 1976–89.
2. Head of state of the People's Republic of Bulgaria, 1971–89.
3. Original title *Comment les démocraties finissent*, Paris, 1983.

policy, and her confidence in the wisdom of the Foreign Office was less than overwhelming.

But even unconventional advisers were fumbling in the dark. In the secretive world of communist affairs it could hardly be otherwise. None of us fully realized at the time the extent of the Polish regime's colonial ingratitude to Moscow after as much as before the imposition of martial law in December 1981. And none of us knew, as we do now, that the Soviet invasion of Afghanistan had been undertaken only after a great deal of anxiety and hesitation in the Soviet leadership itself. There was much else we did not know but had to sound informed about.

It was from an uncertain raft on a fast-flowing stream – and in the total absence of official British knowledge – that Margaret Thatcher's unconventional advisers had to form their judgements and guide the thinking of an unconventional prime minister.

Diary

25 January 1981

Yesterday's working lunch with Margaret Thatcher at Chequers was my first personal contact with the prime minister. We had had some correspondence about making the BBC's foreign-language broadcasts more relevant to the requirements of the 'Cold War' – she had been pressing for a Ukrainian Service which I strongly supported – but we hadn't met.

Lunch was for a group of academics[1] Hugh Thomas[2] had assembled to help the PM with preparing for her visit to newly elected Ronald Reagan. What was our reading of the president's mind? Was there a natural affinity between Reagan and herself? How would Anglo-American relations play out? What sort of policies would emerge from the new administration about the USSR and who were

---

1. Professors Michael (later Sir Michael) Howard, Douglas Johnson, Laurence (later Sir Laurence) Martin, Leonard Schapiro, Dennis Mack Smith, Esmond Wright and myself.

2. Lord Thomas of Swynnerton, Chairman of the Centre for Policy Studies – a Conservative research institute, founded by Margaret Thatcher and Keith Joseph in 1974.

the principal players? Such, in Hugh's words on the telephone, were the questions the PM wanted to have discussed informally. She knew, he said, that we were well-wishers and would listen to us carefully.

I had just returned from Washington and had no time to make preparations, but Hugh assured me that none was required. The PM would bounce off her ideas on us and we'd produce ours. Hugh is a dedicated adviser and very close to her; he knows her ways. His decision to include me in the group was very pleasing.

I arrived a few minutes early. Found a Lotus parked in front and soon met its owner, Mark Thatcher, who came to the lobby to say hello in lieu of his mother. I was the first to arrive – some painful small talk followed. He explained to me the marvels of his car: a turbo-fan Lotus with a high maximum speed. On the new roads he could make it to London and back in less than two hours. I was duly impressed; Mark himself, however, made no impression on me whatever. He gave me a glass of tomato juice; we were not on the same wavelength; we were killing time. Fortunately our embarrassment was short. Wearing a turquoise outfit, the PM walked in. She looked relaxed, self-confident and very attractive. We shook hands. She knew enough about me (Hugh had given her a copy of *Détente*)[1] to ask no time-wasting questions. But when she discovered that Pat[2] and I had spent the night in Amersham, she said: 'Well, had I known that, you could both have stayed here. You must do so next time.' I wonder whether there is going to be one.

She then explained that the great reception room we were chatting in had been renewed under 'Ted' [Heath] who had had the oak panelling restored to its original Elizabethan white. 'Ted' got a grant for it, she added. She thought it looked splendid. So it did.

My first impressions of Margaret Thatcher: she is much softer and more feminine than I gathered from her appearances on television – a man's woman in slow decline. Even her voice – her main weakness in front of the microphone – struck me as low-key and

1. London, 1976.
2. Patricia Urban, author's wife.

inoffensive. She was friendly without being overwhelming, courteous, and inquisitive only within the limits of a warming-up session. In other words: a model hostess. I took to her instantly. The tabloid rags' 'Maggie Rules OK' couldn't have been more right. She had, of course, the long history of this great country house, the legacy of Churchill, and now prime ministerial power on her side, and she obviously knew how to make use of all three. Given what I know about her policies, nothing could delight me more.

As soon as everyone was present, Margaret Thatcher delved into business. What did we think about Poland? Leonard Schapiro and I (the group's two voices on Eastern Europe) said that a Soviet invasion or a hard-line coup of some kind was still very much on the cards. The PM wouldn't go along with that. She couldn't conceive how the Soviets could justify any such move seeing that it would lead to economic penalties, the collapse of *détente* and other undesirable consequences. Leonard and I, however, insisted (and we were in almost total agreement) that a successful Polish defiance would mortally threaten the cohesion of the whole Soviet system and empire.

A setback in economic relations with the West and a further dilution of *détente* were risks the Soviet leaders might be willing to take, we said, but a successful rebellion by Poland was life-threatening. The Kremlin could no more afford it than it could the Hungarian uprising in 1956 or Czech reform-Communism in 1968. The Russians, we tentatively predicted, would invade or organize a *putsch* even at the cost of a bloody showdown with the Poles, risking, if they had to, all the things the prime minister had mentioned. Unwillingly, as I thought, the PM took this on board.

We had a rather convivial time over lunch discussing a wide variety of topics without any organizing principle to make them cohere: the distribution of cabinet posts in the Reagan administration, the advantages and disadvantages of the thirty-year rule on cabinet papers, and the title of Larry Martin's forthcoming Reith Lectures.

'What exactly is the title of your lectures?' Mrs Thatcher wanted to know.

'The role of military power in world affairs' or something very much like it, was Martin's answer.

'Oh, no, no – that's far too learned – far too impenetrable for the run of the mill listener. Can we think of a more appealing title for Larry's lectures?'

So everyone offered improvements, my contribution being 'Hitting them for Six', which raised a laugh.[1]

Martin then spoke about Dick Pipes's[2] surprising absence from the Reagan cabinet. Both he and Schapiro said this was a pity because Dick was not only an outstanding historian but also one of the staunchest critics of the Soviet system in the Reagan camp. Having enjoyed Dick's friendship for many years, I could confirm that. The PM then told us that she had a very full schedule for the coming weeks: in addition to her trip to America to see Reagan, she was down to visit India. Then there was the Commonwealth conference; the Dutch prime minister was coming to London, and so on. But she seemed to thrive on the thought of all these activities.

As soon as the main discussion started I was rather horrified to see that, despite Hugh Thomas's assurance that this would be an off-the-cuff occasion, everyone had a rather neat little presentation tucked up his sleeve. Everyone, that is, except myself. Here we were, heading for a formal conference and I alone had arrived naked!

Coffee was served by a team of WRAFs. We were sitting in a semicircle in front of a huge fire periodically fed by the PM. She was opening and closing windows depending on the whims of the draft under an Elizabethan chimney. Very much at home, she was clearly enjoying the occasion. She was sitting on a treble settee, with Michael Howard at the far end; Hugh Thomas and I were sharing another.

Hugh, in the chair, opened the meeting giving us a thumbnail sketch of the foreign policy issues facing the Reagan team. I felt he

---

1. Laurence Martin's lectures were eventually broadcast under the title of *The Two-Edged Sword – Armed Force in the Modern World*, and published under the same title in London, 1982.

2. Richard Pipes, professor of Russian history, Harvard University.

was basing himself considerably on General Haig's[1] testimony to Congress, of which I had sent him a copy. Last week in Washington I spent the best part of two days watching Haig on television – a great performance by any standard, something we don't often see in inarticulate America.

Larry Martin then briefed us about the issues surrounding the Amex missile system, the wider problems of parity and a number of technical matters I am not qualified to judge. I'm convinced that the missiles will never be put to use, but I approve of them as a threat and a symbol. Was it Frederick the Great who said diplomacy without military power is like music without the instruments? What leaves me absolutely cold is the military 'trade-union' talking impenetrable jargon to the exclusion of the rest of the world. Fortunately, Martin gave it a wide berth.

I for my part said we would be ill-advised to think of American 'national' attitudes in a European framework as though the Americans were a single nation. In reality, unlike the French, or the English, or the Poles, the Americans were a 'nation' only in the sense in which 'national' was used for 'countrywide', but the enduring character of the American melting-pot was more and more open to doubt. Hence American political behaviour was less predictable and more accident-prone than European national attitudes tended to be. The Americans' puzzlement at the survival of European nationalisms was one sign of their otherness. One day (I went on) the Americans may become a single nation, with all its pluses, and especially minuses, for the rest of the world, but that day was not yet.

I went on to suggest that the recent change from indifference to greater firmness in the American attitude to Soviet expansionism should be taken with a pinch of salt. Reagan's rhetoric was much to be applauded, but was his resolve here to stay? Wouldn't American faddism or some unexpected reverse undermine it? America was not of a piece; nor was the US 'government'. A few casualties here, a

---

1. General Alexander Haig, supreme allied commander in Europe, 1974–79; US secretary of state 1981–82.

Congressional countdown there might show America up as the 'paper tiger' the Maoists always said it was.

Then there was also the American press's unpleasant habit of putting the knife into American presidents after a short honeymoon period. Reagan, occupying the position he did on the radical Right of the American spectrum, would be especially vulnerable.

Some of this could be counteracted, at least in the foreign policy field, by close personal understanding between the prime minister and the president. Their policies were similar in both domestic and international affairs. A personal rapport might ensure greater consistency in American attitudes, especially toward the USSR. The Americans seem to have put the trauma of Vietnam behind them. The prime minister's clarity of understanding and resolve could strengthen the president's hand, I concluded.

I was then asked to talk about *détente*. East and West had conflicting interpretations of this elusive notion, I said. Western public opinion took it to mean overall peace; the Kremlin, by contrast, never tired of telling us that while a shooting war had to be avoided, in the battle of ideas there could be no peaceful coexistence between 'capitalism' and 'socialism'. But, I said, this was a challenge we should welcome. Our ideas were sound and had stood the test of time. Democracy and individual freedom had an appeal way beyond the borders of the Western world. The Soviets, on the other hand, had created a slum empire built on propaganda and coercion. But, I went on, in order to react to the Soviet challenge with success, we needed something like an overall Western information policy.

The PM interjected: did I mean countering subversion?

That would, of course, be included, I replied, but it was more important to counter Moscow's attempt to capture the 'hearts and minds' of people worldwide. To do so, we would have to fine-tune and coordinate our articulations. Admittedly, it was difficult to make 'propaganda' on behalf of democracy without making nonsense of it, and the Americans felt especially inhibited, but it could be done and had been done with success *vis-à-vis* both Hitler and Stalin. Now, in the age of *détente*, new and more subtle approaches were called for. Here was something Britain could initiate and the Reagan administration might consider with considerable sympathy.

The PM was nodding her approval.

Next Douglas Johnson spoke about the domestic scene in France. He is a man of immense reading and sophistication but said little we didn't know from the papers. Dennis Mack Smith held forth about the chaos prevailing in Christian Democratic quarters in Italy. He seemed to have no answers to Italy's continuing afflictions. Who has? I volunteered a bit of information I had recently garnered from Count Luigi Rossi, a Christian Democratic deputy and member of the Martini Rossi tribe. Rossi told me (I related) that the Italian Christian Democrats were now suffering from that terminal disease of all political parties: the loss of confidence that they had the right to govern.

'I'm a little reluctant to quote Lenin in this company,' I said, 'but he had a great piece of truth on his side when he observed that such loss of self-confidence was a prelude to and a precondition of revolution.' And I wondered whether the Italian conservatives quite understood where demoralization and self-abdication might take their country. Mack Smith answered that the Italian situation was desperate but not serious – an *aperçu* that has done well for Italy for a great many years and will probably go on doing well for many more.

While all this was going on, the PM was taking notes, asking every now and then for clarification, but speaking little.

With the formal session over, tea was served and an entertaining free-for-all began. MT was wondering what might have motivated Brezhnev and the other Soviet leaders to intervene in Afghanistan. Why on earth did they do it? Moscow had things pretty well under control; there was no great threat coming from that country. The Soviets must have realized that they would be jeopardizing *détente*, damaging their standing in the Third World, undermining their international propaganda, and putting the clock back in East–West economic relations. Were they blind to their own interests? Were they being driven by some consideration we knew nothing about?[1]

A number of explanations were offered, the fear of Islamic fundamentalism in the region being the main one. I came up with a view
that is central to my thinking about Soviet attitudes to the non-
communist world: communist power, once ensconced, must never be
surrendered. This is and has always been an article of faith in the
Kremlin's philosophy. It followed almost organically from the Tsars'
long and relentless expansionism. The Russians, I said, regarded the
extension of their power to Afghanistan via Marxism-Leninism as a
symbol of the legitimacy of their message for mankind and especially
the Third World. They were determined to show that once a country
had walked down the road of 'socialism' with Soviet support, and
then fell on hard times, it could always count on Soviet protection.
The march of history could not be reversed. Afghanistan, I said,
was the application of the Brezhnev doctrine to Asian conditions,
with serious implications for Western security. The Great Game was
on again; the same warm-water ports as had figured in the calculations of the Tsars were the ultimate objectives of the Soviet leaders
too.

The prime minister then switched her anxiety to subversion in
the British media. A Sunday television interview had deeply upset
her. Why are there so many subversives in our media? Why all the
left-inspired carping and scepticism? Why the Pavlovian approval of
the anti-Western position in almost any argument? Were our com-
municators simply ignorant? Was there method – or Soviet disinformation – in their madness?

Michael Howard said it would be an error to assume that such
people were all communists or Soviet agents of influence. Hostility
to 'official' policies, and conservative policies in particular, was
deeply embedded in Western culture. England was no exception.

---

1. Documents declassified in Russia in the early 1990s show that between
March and December 1979, Brezhnev, Kosygin, Andropov, Gromyko and the
other Soviet leaders were first extremely reluctant to intervene in Afghanistan
precisely for the reasons Margaret Thatcher listed in this discussion. See 'Docu-
mentation', Cold War International History Project, *Bulletin*, no. 4, Washington
DC, Fall 1994, pp. 70–6.

Cultivating a sceptical 'show-me' frame of mind, which British schools and universities, too, were rightly encouraging, moved many of the young, even when they were no longer so young, to embrace left-wing causes. The phenomenon was worldwide – a vast topic well worth a mass in its own right, he noted.

I added, agreeing with everything Howard had said, that the kind of subversion the prime minister had in mind, and especially the kind of apologia offered to whitewash Soviet policies, were an intellectual fashion at the moment which reason and evidence alone could not dent. 'How do I cause maximum discomfort and annoyance to our rulers?' was the real motivation of the carpers. What we had to aim for was to make that intellectual fashion socially unacceptable. But that was a task for the distant future and not easy to prescribe for. Happily, the blindly obedient fellow-travellers were extinct – the milder variety, too, would soon be on their way out.

Here Schapiro butted in to say that while Soviet disinformation was very active and our journalistic ill-wishers and innocents were soft touches, it would be a mistake to hold disinformation solely or even mainly responsible for bias in the media. He agreed that the lopsidedness of the culture of the young was principally responsible, but the young had a habit of growing up and shedding their illusions. For an old man, however, he added with a smile, that was of course small consolation.

We concluded that education was the long-term answer to our problem, but none of us said how that answer could be arrived at without undoing much that had happened in Western thinking since the Enlightenment. *We* knew that the Soviet system was rotten to the core, but it was exceptionally difficult to communicate that knowledge to closed minds. An influential segment of the Western intelligentsia was in the grips of a false consciousness, and that was a notoriously hard thing to defeat.

Let me add here in parentheses that Schapiro himself and his excellent team at the London School of Economics are Britain's most powerful nucleus of sane judgement of the Soviet Union. The PM is fully aware of this.

We then fell to talking about British troop strengths in Germany. The PM said ideally she would like to take some of our troops out to reduce cost and fill in the gaps elsewhere. What did we think?

I made a few remarks to the effect that a form of leave-us-out-of-it (*ohne uns*) mentality was riding high on the German Left, notably in the ranks of the radical wing of the SPD, but not only there. Any sign of a UK or American withdrawal would be read as a signal of endorsement of a non-aligned German future, which was not in the Western interest. The PM said she knew well enough that right now even a partial withdrawal would be politically impossible, but under a different set of conditions our troops – with their professional excellence of which she was proud – could be put to better use in other parts of the world. In Germany, they were immobilized.

'Isn't it curious', she went on in a tone of disapproval, 'how strong the Franco-German axis has become, and how well Giscard[1] and Schmidt[2] are getting along with each other? It's extraordinary! They seem to hit it off; they are personal friends and speak the same sort of language' (she didn't say it was English).

She then held up her arms vertically: 'You see, this here on one side is Schmidt, and that on the other is Giscard. Standing separately, they are strong but not excessively strong. But when they stand together like this' – and she made an inverted V sign with her arms like twin pillars supporting a bridge – 'they have immense influence; they shape European policy and are a powerful factor on the world scene.' She was clearly displeased with so much Franco-German understanding.

'But wasn't Franco-German reconciliation and partnership what Churchill urged us to promote in his Zurich speech in 1946?' Schapiro interjected.

'And isn't that a very good thing for the peace of Europe?' I added.

---

1. Valéry Giscard d'Estaing, president of France, 1974–81.
2. Helmut Schmidt, chancellor of the German Federal Republic, 1974–82.

The PM didn't respond.

She was especially down on French behaviour. The French, she said, were marching out of step with us on any number of issues: they sell arms by hook or by crook, they oppose wherever they can American leadership, they refuse to rejoin NATO, they pursue their selfish interests in *détente* and are generally bloody minded. And do you know why? Because they consider such policies as symbols of French virility! That's what it is: French virility. How absurd can they get!

None of us interfered with her train of thought.

We broke up at 5.30. It was a long lunch. Margaret Thatcher said she found our 'seminar' highly stimulating. The ideas seeded would go on germinating in her mind. We had offered perspectives she was not getting from civil servants. The Foreign Office briefs went through several sieves before they reached her and did not therefore represent a wide enough spectrum of views. Our correctives, she said, were invaluable.

'Incidentally,' she went on, 'all these ideas will vanish from our minds unless we have them on paper. So if anyone wants to volunteer to put his thoughts in writing he should do so and let me have his paper through Hugh.'

But there were no volunteers. I thought her request was too general to mobilize us. When it came to saying farewell, however, Michael Howard suddenly volunteered me rather than himself.

'It might be useful, prime minister, if we could persuade George to let us have a short paper on information policy and his concept of an ideological counter-offensive.' MT looked at me questioningly. 'I'd be happy to write a paper for you, prime minister,' I said.

As we lined up in the lobby to shake hands, MT said with a genial smile: 'And you will write that memorandum for me, won't you? It would be very helpful if I could have it before my departure for America.' I assured her that she would have it in time and that I would write it with pleasure.

I left Chequers feeling that this highly intelligent well-informed and resolute lady would make mincemeat of the American leader-

26

ship. What a pleasure to see a person of ideas in charge of declining Britain!

America is immensely more powerful than this country, but Britain has an exceptional leader. Greeks to the Romans again, in the phrase of Harold Macmillan? I rather doubt it, but the information we have about the president's conception of his role leads me to believe that he sees himself as chairman of a board of governors and not a hands-on manager of the kind European prime ministers (and some European presidents) tend to be and have to be. Nor does he appear to suffer from an excess of reading or any marked thirst for the more complicated sorts of information.

Mrs T, on the other hand, appears to enjoy enormously the highways and byways of ideas and values her guides on her journey. I'd be surprised if the president could keep up with the lady. For all these reasons, she must be careful not to embarrass him. But I think she is aware of that. On the large questions of the day, and especially on Western policy *vis-à-vis* the Soviet Union, Reagan's mind is made up and close to the views of Margaret Thatcher. To identify just how close their views may be was probably the main purpose of yesterday's meeting, but for me at least the byways were more fascinating.

26 January 1981

Spoke to Hugh Thomas on the phone. He feels Chequers went well. The PM was pleased. He has never seen her quite so relaxed. He wants me to write my piece by Friday week; he will then put it in the PM's 'Friday box' for Saturday reading. This I will do, and I'll also attach to this Diary whatever I will have written.

29 January 1981

Have rushed out a note on information policy. It may strike the PM – and will certainly strike the Foreign Office crowd if they are ever shown it – as wildly out of tune with the ways of sedate government.

But, with the PM suspicious of Foreign Office advice in any case, it can hardly make things worse. My suggestion for a media-watch would also line up the press and TV against us, although some watching by private groups is already in progress. I'm sure Mrs T will keep my note under wraps – or so I would advise her – until she decides to take action. Here is what I'm sending her through Hugh Thomas, to be dated 1 February 1981:

A NOTE ON INFORMATION POLICY

I will confine this brief report and my tentative recommendations to three, somewhat arbitrarily defined, areas: (1) public morale and political leadership, (2) disinformation, loaded reporting and subversion through the press, radio and television, and (3) means of a Western ideological counter-offensive *vis-à-vis* the Soviet Union. They apply *mutatis mutandis* to the US as much as to Britain. I will use telegraphic language to condense my meaning wherever possible.

(1) Both British and American society are in a state of declining moral health. Spiritual disorientation, the loss of our ability to tell true values from non-values, the impairment of our sense of priorities, the weakening of our perception of what constitutes human dignity and a worth-while life, the debasement of the idea of the university, the erosion of the frontiers between law and lawlessness are some of the more obvious symptoms.

No one has yet made a convincing analysis of what makes for national morale, yet we can at once recognize a state of affairs in which morale is low or lost and the public sluggish to respond to leadership, or indeed inhibits the rise or maintenance of leadership.

To some extent all Western societies suffer from a loss of morale. In Britain it takes principally the form of poor work ethic and low motivation; in Germany a sense of collective fear of the future; in America a perplexity at the disappearance of 'American exceptionalism' and the seeming unmanageability of most of America's internal and world problems. All Western countries share a creeping sense of helplessness in the face of an apparently unstoppable Soviet Union and the turbulent and impenetrable politics of the Third World.

Whether such attitudes are the consequences of satiety and too much affluence, the 'something for nothing' mentality of the welfare state, or the excessive privatization of life and the ensuing reluctance to make sacrifices for the national good, has little bearing on the conclusion that we are faced with a malignancy that threatens our survival.

We may, of course, take some comfort from the fact that civilian – though not military – morale in the Soviet Union and Eastern Europe is a great deal worse, and the fabric of society a great deal more brittle. Yet the morale sustaining the performance of our new industrial rivals in the 'Confucian cultural belt' of the world – Japan, South Korea, Taiwan, Singapore and increasingly China – is high and the cohesiveness of their industrial civilization robust.

No one can offer a cure-all for so widespread a malaise. Yet we have reason to think that the worst of the disease is over. Conservative victory at the last British general election, and more recently the election of President Reagan in the US, strike me as significant reassertions of the political will and signs of a much greater public readiness to overcome those feelings of self-doubt, impotence and (as in the case of America) crises of guilt and identity, which have done so much to undermine our social cohesion and our willingness to stand up for our way of life.

Both the British and American people admire strong leadership, simple language and desire a share in their leaders' thoughts. They like strength even if it implies temporary hardship; simplicity even if they have reason to suspect that the real world is one of utmost complexity; and 'intimacy' even if certain media-sophisticates decry it as moralizing, patronizing or simple-minded.

President Carter's failure was in large part due to his own and his Administration's failure to communicate. His leadership was hesitant, his public presentation of America's problems almost as complex as the problems themselves, and his public persona divorced from any sense of immediacy or intimacy. He was patently not there with the answers – he was part of the problem himself. In an age of television, the public has an unerring eye for self-doubt and indecision.

The British prime minister is conspicuous by suffering from none of these handicaps. Her strong leadership is widely admired, not least – though grudgingly – by her adversaries. We have reason to assume that President Reagan, too, will lead the nation as well as his government, that he will simplify whenever simplification is called for, and communicate to the hearts of the American public.

These are considerable assets. How do we turn them to good account in the context of Britain's particular problems?

We need, or so it seems to me, a variety of 'self-confidence-building' and 'self-discipline-building' measures at several levels of application. We are familiar enough with the obstacles at the level of the press, radio and television.

The 'professional deformation' of media-reporting is one debilitating factor (almost as intractable in this country as it is in America). The masochistic public taste for a daily intake of bad news is another. The cultural 'alienation' of part of the British public from the values of industrial civilization is a third. There are others.

I would envisage, as a short-term emergency measure, a series of television fireside chats – somewhat on the FDR pattern – probably by the prime minister herself. The edge, though not the tone, of these talks would be frankly didactic, their language simple and their message of immediate appeal. They would deal with themes such as:

— the individual's duties to himself, his family and his community;
— the self-rewarding nature of work well done;
— the needs of discipline, punctuality and quality-consciousness in an export-oriented economy;
— unemployment as a time for learning new skills and extending qualifications;
— increasing the individual's life-chances in a depersonalizing industrial environment;
— the needs and satisfactions of recurrent (continuing) education, and the like.

All this may seem a puny answer to a formidable problem, and so it is. Undoubtedly, a more searching study would yield more promising long-term recommendations. I am persuaded that the roots of our poor industrial ethos and general under-motivation are historical and cultural rather than just economic. Hence our remedies, too, must attack the problem at that level. That even so modest a programme must necessarily exceed the time-horizon of a single government is true, but somewhere a beginning has to be made.

(2) Misrepresentation and subversive reporting by the mass media is the hardest nut to crack. The Western countries are officially at peace with the Soviet Union, yet the Soviet Union pursues its particular mixture of neither-war-nor-peace policy. It enjoys, in its information policy, all the advantages accruing to a totalitarian power at war, whereas

we suffer from all the restrictions of a parliamentary democratic order at peace. But we can shoot back.

It would be a mistake to think that tendentious reporting and disinformation are the direct outcome of subversion by Soviet agencies or the British far left. I have no doubt that some biased reporting *is* due to infiltration by one or the other, but the bulk of distorted reportage must be ascribed to the heavily slanted social, educational and intellectual milieu, and the particular chic, of the last two decades. It is a long-term social and intellectual problem which calls for long-term solutions.

Short of writing a report on national education policy, I would suggest:

— continuing government pressure on the media, especially the BBC, to justify various pieces of television reportage;
— the encouragement of parliamentary demand for a White Paper (or its equivalent) on BBC information policy;
— some form of special grant to be made available to left-wing reporters to spend time in the Soviet Union – they will return cured;
— covert or private financial support for a monthly review of media misrepresentation;
— moral and, wherever appropriate, financial encouragement of private organizations which have acted as watchdogs in the past or seem likely to do so in the future.

(3) Here we would do well to take a leaf out of the communist book and think in terms of some combination of overt and covert action. On the level of the first, I would attach great importance to a campaign of 'ideological' enlightenment of the Western public itself. Carrying the cultural/ideological counter-offensive to the doorstep of our adversaries presupposes a firm home base. This is more easily obtained in Britain than in the US but should, in the prevailing American atmosphere, be well within the grasp of the Reagan administration too. Our underlying theme should be the rejection of the Marxist idea that history follows some preordained course, with the Western 'bourgeois' countries as the inevitable losers. I would envisage a number of high-level articulations, preferably by the prime minister and the US president, spelling out:

— the expansion of Soviet power v. British, French and Dutch decolonization since 1945;

31

— the Soviet interpretation of 'peace' and 'war';
— the Soviet view of 'national liberation' movements;
— the 'Brezhnev doctrine' of limited sovereignty;
— the fragile structure of the (non-binding) Helsinki Agreement;
— the pitfalls of *détente*;
— the contribution of Western credits and trade to the expansion of Soviet power;
— the Soviet interpretation of trade-union rights, freedom of the press, assembly, opinion and jurisdiction;
— the character of Soviet propaganda, disinformation and subversion.

I would, furthermore, recommend institutional initiatives in a number of areas at the level of policy interpretation and intelligence. I am aware that some of these may prove incompatible with considerations entertained by the government but not known to myself. Let me state them all the same.

a) The overt establishment of 'free radios' (somewhat on the pattern of Radio Free Europe/Radio Liberty) as alternative home services for Cuba, Libya, Angola, Ethiopa, South Yemen, Vietnam, Cambodia, North Korea and Afghanistan.
b) Clandestine broadcasting to the Ukraine, the Baltic states, Georgia, Central Asia, Cuba, Libya and Afghanistan.
c) Political, intelligence and financial support for opposition groups in some or all of the above.
d) Moral and financial support of various international groups, organizations and journals working in the same direction and the encouragement of new ones.
e) Recognition and support of an Afghan Government or Committee in Exile. Open support for the Afghan freedom fighters.
f) Establishment of a 'BBC Third World Service'.
g) Establishment of a small body of scholars and intelligence experts to suggest ways of bridging the gap between Western cultural attitudes and the expectations of those modernizing groups within Islam which appear to be willing to come to terms with the West.
h) An 'Office of Information Policy' under American or Anglo-American auspices to manage suitable sections of the above.

Inevitably the US would have to assume the principal political and financial responsibility for this tentative programme. Nevertheless, it would be a convincing gesture of allied solidarity – and a means of acquiring probably disproportionate British influence – if the British Government offered expertise, political and intelligence cooperation and some financial support.

A word in conclusion about American psychology. Although President Reagan and his team do not appear to be lacking self-confidence, it is a safe assumption that the American people have not yet completely emerged from the trauma and self-mortification of Watergate and Vietnam. They are constantly in search of assurance that they are not alone in a hostile and chaotic world.

The prime minister will be the first of the new president's major foreign visitors. Her reputation among the leaders of the new administration is high. So is Britain's reputation for political experience and wisdom. Anglo-American consanguinity is close to the heart of the president. The prime minister, I am certain, will be welcomed as a close ally – indeed probably the closest. Any public expression on her part of solidarity with America's impending new departures (such as sharing the US burden in the Persian Gulf area) should help to still the American people's vestigial fears of isolation.

CHAPTER 2

Midwife to Two
Speeches

By the summer of 1983, with victory in the Falklands War and a second electoral triumph behind her, Margaret Thatcher had established herself on the national and international scene as a charismatic stateswoman. Her affinity and friendship with Ronald Reagan were now facts rather than aspirations. Her economic radicalism was making converts throughout the world, and even under-performing Britain was shaken out of its torpor. Soviet expansionism was about to be checked by the American arms build-up and NATO's deployment of intermediate-range nuclear forces. At the United Nations and in the eyes of world public opinion, Moscow was in the dock because of the unprovoked destruction of a South Korean airliner.

Two major speeches Margaret Thatcher had been committed to make at the end of September – one in the United States and another in Canada – were now waiting to be drafted. She could hardly have wished for a more propitious environment. 'Churchillian' in mood and vocabulary, one of the two speeches was eventually widely rumoured to have come from the pens of Lord Thomas and myself – and so much of it did. Speaking for myself only, I provided some 'Churchillian' words and metaphors for Margaret Thatcher, not because I believed her to be quite of Churchillian stature – though my respect for her was immense – but rather because I thought she was the most persuasive and eye-catching representative of the new Western determination to stop the Soviet Union. After the West's humiliating retreats and vacillations in the Carter period and under *détente*, she was a universal symbol of hope. I knew she was not for turning.

Diary

18/19 September 1983

A wing-commander of the WRAF[1] showed me into the white parlour [of Chequers] where I found the prime minister, Hugh Thomas and John Coles[2] of the Foreign Office well into our topic. My driver had missed a turning near Amersham. I was slightly late. I offered my apologies. The PM stood up to welcome me.

I felt she looked a bit the worse for wear after her eye operation, but I soon discovered that her spirit and stamina were unaffected. She was to wear us out with her finely targeted curiosity before the day was out. 'We were just saying that you'd be arriving between 10.30 and 10.45,' she said with a smile, trying to put me out of any embarrassment; 'driving here from Sussex one can never forecast the exact time of arrival. You got here in fact four minutes before our parameter.'

Without further ado, holding some *Encounter*[3] galleys in her hands, the PM launched into an animated, page-by-page discussion – interpretation would be a better word – of my conversation with Jeane Kirkpatrick.[4] This 'exegesis' of my own text rather amused me. A few days ago I had heard from Hugh Thomas that the PM had received a copy of the Kirkpatrick–Urban materials from Charlie Douglas-Home,[5] but I had no idea that she wanted to make use of them.

Coffee was brought in; Hugh was spread out in a wing-chair near the fireplace, Coles had taken up position on a settee some distance away with a pad on his knee, and the PM was at the window. I must have been fumbling in my clumsy way with my coffee-cup, for she

---

1. Women's Royal Air Force.

2. Later Sir John Coles, head of the diplomatic service; permanent under-secretary of state.

3. Anglo-American journal.

4. Jeane J. Kirkpatrick, United States ambassador to the United Nations; member of the Reagan cabinet.

5. Editor of *The Times*, 1982–85.

rose and pulled up a small table next to my chair with a maternal gesture: '*That* should be better,' she said, trying to put me at my ease. 'Ease' came later in the day, but the first hour with Britain's formidable prime minister was anything but relaxing. In one sense, I was, of course, profoundly gratified. Planning a speech with Margaret Thatcher at Chequers seemed a long way away from my childhood habitat in Balatonalmádi-Öreghegy.[1] In another, however, I was slightly apprehensive: could I impart anything to this great lady she didn't know already?

Mrs Thatcher then began to explain why she had sent for me. A few days ago, she said, she told Charlie Douglas-Home that she was looking for fresh ideas for two important speeches she was about to make – one in the US, another in Canada. The first was to be her acceptance speech at the Winston Churchill Award dinner in Washington, the second in the Canadian Parliament. Could he help? Charlie apparently had the galley proofs of my *Encounter* piece with him (he was going to publish extracts in *The Times*), so he handed them to the PM with the comment that he had been much inspired and so perhaps might she.

'Well, I have now carefully read the whole long piece, and I must tell you I found it exceptionally interesting. It is full of insights of the sort close to my thinking – not only on the part of Kirkpatrick, but every bit as much on your side too. As a matter of fact, there are odd words and phrases in what Kirkpatrick says (I'll come to those later) I *don't* agree with, but most of it is sound, and I found several of your entries especially congenial.' She then showed me how she had underlined whole passages in the galleys to stress her agreement with various arguments Jeane and I had fielded. She was by now in full flood. I was happily surprised by her obvious enjoyment of the occasion and her enthusiasm. Hugh had told me that talking business with the PM was an intellectual experience second to none. 'Don't make elaborate preparations,' he had said, 'just spin off some of your ideas and let's see where we go. She loves having

---

1. Summer home of author's family in Hungary.

a free argument.' And so it proved to be. It didn't take me long to feel that I was temperamentally aligned with the PM whatever the precise subject of the argument.

Once again, I found Margaret Thatcher an attractive lady. She was exuding a dignified, low-key, but very consciously cultivated kind of charm. Now in her fifties, she has nevertheless retained the movements, the legs and walk of a young woman. She is clearly aware that men will do things for her they might not do so willingly for another man. I may be one of them. But far from taking away from her authority, her feminine qualities seem to be adding to it. After a triumphant re-election, her honeymoon with the British people is unclouded.

'One of the ideas that struck me most in your talk with Kirkpatrick', she went on, 'was what you say here about the Western democracies being the home of the thinking and the conscience of the entire planet. Too true.' She then read out a large part of one of my entries:

> Somewhere at the back of the mind of almost every communist there lurks a feeling that the Soviet system is an aberration, and that normality, with its unregulated variety, sanity, compassion, safety-nets, and human satisfactions, is to be had in the West only. Communists I have known certainly conduct themselves on the unspoken assumption that 'somewhere out there' capitalism and democracy – like some much abused but safe parental home – is being quietly kept in a state of good repair, to which they can return when Utopia has turned sour or a visit to the dentist is due ... It is in the democratic West that the world's conscience is located; and it is the West that does the entire world's creative thinking. 'You in the West have a special duty because you are free,' a Hungarian Catholic poet[1] told me in Budapest in the late 1960s. 'That freedom is both a blessing and a burden, for it makes you spiritually responsible for the whole of humanity ... The

---

1. János Pilinszky. His collected poems appeared in English in 1989 in a translation by János Csokits and Ted Hughes under the title *The Desert of Love*.

Communist East has been as barren of creative thinking as it has been of creative art and technological innovation.'[1]

That's good, very good,' the PM exclaimed.

'Well,' she went on, 'I'd like to use this theme in some form in one of my American speeches. It is a striking truth. We have to underline it. It is our job to say these things to the Soviets and the world. That is, by the way, why I don't *always* agree with Jeane Kirkpatrick. Repeatedly in this piece she talks about the Kremlin's "ideological aggression". She says the Soviets are guilty of it. But that's wrong. Physical aggression would be a different matter, but I can see nothing wrong with the Russians using every word in the dictionary to press upon the world their point of view – no matter how mistaken and mendacious it may be. The problem is on our side. We must *answer back* and take the offensive. Surely, as free and creative nations, we have the better opportunities and the more convincing arguments. Surely we have the resources to back us up. Why don't we use them? "Ideological aggression" simply means that the communists are waging a verbal war against us. Right – so should *we* against *them*.'

This was my own strongly held view too. We were warming to our main theme. I said the Soviet principle of 'peaceful coexistence' expressly encourages us to fight the battle of symbols and ideas with all peaceful means at our disposal. I would incorporate words to that effect in the draft of her American speech. The Kremlin, I said, works on the principle of 'what is mine is mine – what is yours is negotiable'. The nice thing, I said, about the Soviet concept of 'peaceful coexistence' is that it applies only to countries with 'antagonistic' social systems: America and the USSR should not go to war with each other. Between 'fraternal' states of the 'socialist' community, however, 'peaceful coexistence' does not apply. The 'socialist' states are free to be 'assisted' by other socialist states under 'proletarian internationalism', and that is the doctrine under which

---

1. Jeane Kirkpatrick and George Urban, 'American Foreign Policy in a Cold Climate', *Encounter*, November 1983, pp. 23–4.

Czechoslovakia was invaded in 1968. The PM laughed. We need not worry too much about attacks from the Left, I went on; Andropov himself has spoken about a worldwide contest for hearts and minds. We are simply fighting our corner. Again, Mrs Thatcher picked up the theme of a counter-offensive with alacrity: 'I'm perfectly prepared to fight that battle – we've got all the truth on our side and all the right arguments; we've got everything going for us.'

The PM then suggested that we should make some reference in 'our' draft (we were now sharing an enterprise) to President Reagan's forceful speech to the joint Houses of Parliament at Windsor Castle (8 June 1982). This was Reagan's signal for a Western ideological counter-offensive, and I had given it prominence in my talk with Jeane Kirkpatrick. She continued:

'You summarized Reagan's speech in eight points and that brought out its great significance. I was there in Windsor listening to Reagan with rapt attention, but I don't think it crossed my mind that the president was making a fighting, ideological speech that would change Western policy. Reagan was making jokes, and he was reading his words in such a mellifluous way, with such a natural, sweet expression on his face, that I did not quite catch the tremendous significance of what he was saying. It's as well you've brought it out.'

'There is something else about the Kirkpatrick bits I didn't like,' she went on. 'She talks at one point about the military posture of the *United States*. That's wrong. What she ought to have said was the military posture of the *Alliance*, the Atlantic Alliance, of NATO. It is outrageous to imply that the Americans are alone in this game. We're all in it; we're all part of it, and it's quite wrong for the Americans to throw their weight around and to imply that we are just satellites.'

Mrs Thatcher's strong words came as a surprise to me, though not a complete surprise. She was (wrongly in my view) upset recently about American pressure to stop European gas-pipeline deliveries to the Soviet Union. The Americans must have conducted themselves with very little finesse if they've managed to alienate Margaret

Thatcher, a more pro-American politician than whom we haven't got in the whole of Europe. What I ought to have observed at this point – but didn't – was that Britain was, indeed, an American 'client state', but, for one reason or another, a perfectly willing one. It was clear from the prime minister's tone that, despite her splendid personal understanding and ideological solidarity with Reagan, there is a lot of tension between the two governments, and the cause of that tension appears to be, in the British view at any rate, the Americans' overbearing style in dealing with their partners.

I found the prime minister's energy most impressive. She would flit from topic to topic in search of an incandescent idea or meaningful phrase. Her questions went always to the heart of things, and even where she wasn't fully informed, her sense of where she had to look for connections and what these might be was faultless. We did agree on virtually everything as far as ideas for her two speeches were concerned, and that, of course, helped enormously.

Sitting there with her and Hugh Thomas, I reflected what a great daughter of the English nation this woman is. Even those who curse her must recognize that she out-thinks, outshines and outdoes all her political rivals and (more dangerously) her political supporters too. What is it that makes her into what she is? The ability to think systematically, of course; the rapid assimilation and marshalling of what she needs for her purposes, of course; relentless hard work, of course; but beyond these she has the ability to identify passionately with her chosen course of action, and she is fuelled by an often ruthless drive to project her convictions on to others. A formidable combination.

But aren't these the qualities that also make for dictators and autocrats? Not quite. Maurice Cranston[1] once argued to me that what distinguishes a great leader in a democracy from a Stalin or a Hitler is the taming and civilizing process the democratic leader has to go through in our schools, clubs and universities. He thought the

---

1. Maurice William Cranston, philosopher, formerly professor of politics at the London School of Economics.

very ambitious, including the very wicked, would eventually always get to the top, but we could prevent them from putting their more mischievous ideas into practice by subjecting them in time to the restraining ethic of democracy. 'The right measure of things' would stay their hand. Margaret Thatcher, I reflected, is convincing proof that Cranston was right. In another age and in another national context, she may well have become a despot. The raw ingredients are all there. But in England, in the 1980s, she struck me, for one, as an agent of rejuvenation rather than crude authority, and a symbol of the re-emergence of qualities we have been missing here since the war. The potential extremes in her character have been held in check by English culture.

I am not sure how much the PM likes public praise of her exceptional qualities, but privately she does enjoy it. I certainly said things at Chequers that visibly pleased her; and when Hugh Thomas eulogizes her (as he invariably does) at the Centre for Policy Studies annual general meetings, she does not demur. Far from it.

It was the discussion of her qualities as a leader that moved her to talk about her need of speech-writing assistance. 'I'm not lost for words when it's a question of arguing face-to-face with a high-powered interviewer. I like the give-and-take – wham, wham! I'm stimulated, and perhaps those opposing me are stimulated too. That's how ideas are generated. But when it comes to writing down a speech, I don't like doing it. I find it awkward and rather difficult. I'm much happier with live work. Now, once a speech has been written for me, I've got something to sink my teeth into; I can recast it, I can reorganize it. I can throw out a paragraph, bring in a bit from someone else's draft, rephrase the language and taste the words I'm going to use. It's most important that the words on your lips are *your* words, that they express *your* feelings from the pit of your guts, that they mirror the stuff of which you are made. That is why I need help. Once I've got that, I revivify the argument, I recycle the thinking and make them my own. But I must first have a text in front of me.'

'Well,' I said, 'I certainly got the impression, Prime Minister, that in your television interviews you showed up extremely well, even when you had to present a case *solo*, without helpful irritants.'

'It depends,' she said, 'I don't mind doing those. In interviews, I like to think I can hold my own.'

'You are too modest,' I answered, and I brought up an interview she had given Brian Walden[1] on military matters before the last general election. This was a splendid occasion and an absolute election winner – not that she needed this to win the election. 'In that interview with Walden,' I went on, 'you came out magnificently.'

The PM looked pleased but remained unsmiling. She cast her eyes over the furniture, inspected the carpet, then looked at me again: 'I'm *so* glad to hear that you thought so. That's praise indeed.'

'That's what *everyone* thought,' I said, 'the interview was a triumph.'

'But do you know how I did it?' she went on. 'I mobilized everyone who could possibly help me. I called in the best brains from government departments – the Foreign Office, the Ministry of Defence, the General Staff, the Treasury – they all had to come and advise me, putting before me every scrap of information I might need under Walden's barrage. During the dry runs I insisted on mounting, they put the trickiest questions to me and I had to answer them thinking on my feet. Also, I read all the relevant papers, which were legion. I was determined not to be tripped up or cornered by Brian Walden. That's the background to the interview you liked so much. There was a lot of homework in it, you know.'

'The public does not realize how much preparation goes into such seemingly effortless talks on television,' I said. 'But you did make it look splendidly effortless, and you had a rather chivalrous challenger in Walden. Without trying to compare myself to the British prime minister,' I went on, 'I am myself in the habit of making elaborate preparations for the colloquies you have read. The one you are holding in your hands at the moment was also preceded by considerable preparation.'

---

1. Television presenter, former Labour MP.

As the conversation went on, MT also impressed me as a lady of considerable learning. How does she find the time to do all her reading? She is up to date on the latest literature on political theory, military, economic and social affairs, and even the major periodicals. She reads *Encounter*, *Commentary*[1] and, more important, she can deploy what she's read – a whole new departure from the pre-Thatcher, stick-in-the-mud type of conservatism. 'Intellectual' is no longer a pejorative noun in English usage inside the confines of the Thatcher camp. The PM even threw a quotation at me from *Antigone* – and she was excusing herself that she could no longer remember it in Greek.

My impression is that some of her increasingly numerous contacts with intellectuals, speech-writers and the like have more than a practical purpose: she may be working on her image in history as a great stateswoman surrounded and respected by the leading brains of her time. A court of the Medici adorned by the uncrowned heads of the arts and sciences? Perhaps. Alas, the line between advisers and courtiers has always been a thin one. So it is now. There *are* courtiers in her environment (I shall not name them), but she has also managed to capture the goodwill, even the admiration, of many an egghead whom I would normally expect to see on the other side. An invitation to No. 10 or Chequers has wonderful powers of healing the spirit of alienation and disarming certain members of the left.

Business was suspended over lunch – to the extent that was possible in the presence of MT. There were just the four of us: the PM, Hugh Thomas, John Coles and myself. Our table talk centred on the peculiarities of Soviet 'sensitivity' – in other words: why are the Russians so prickly and bloody-minded? – but only after we had listened to the prime minister's complaint about the Chequers trustees, who were apparently reluctant to allow a tennis court to be laid out for her daughter Carol. And Carol was so anxious to have somewhere to play! We had chicken broth, sauté of beef and raspberry fool, with San Patricio and Burgundy.

---

1. US journal.

Anecdotes were traded about Soviet paranoia. My contribution was a story from the Soviet studies grapevine: 'An American visitor is shown round Moscow by his Russian host. He is given a tour of the marble halls and statues of one of the Moscow metro stations with its spotless floors and neon lighting. "This is the world's technologically most sophisticated, most reliably built and most beautiful underground system," the Russian tells his visitor; "Every two minutes on the dot a train pulls up and whisks you off at speed to your destination." So they stay on the platform expecting the next train. Two minutes pass but there is no train; then six minutes – no train; then ten minutes – still no train. Eventually the American turns to his host: "Well, we've been standing here for twenty minutes and there hasn't been a single train." Whereupon Soviet Man turns on his guest, wagging a finger: "But *you* in America persecute the black man!"'

The PM seemed to enjoy my story and said she would retell it. After lunch we got down to detailed business. The PM was full of self-confidence. Two speeches had to be prepared, she said. Coles had already volunteered to have a go at the Canadian speech based on the ideas we were discussing. Could Hugh and I find the time to help her with a draft for the Churchill Award address? She'd be most grateful.

We agreed that what was needed was a statesman-like speech, short on detail, Churchillian in tone and carrying a principled message. 'The West and the Soviet Union' was to be our topic, but beyond that we were free to write whatever we thought was right.

We want to start off, I said, by depicting the character of the Soviet system and telling the public what sort of an enemy, what sort of a regime we are facing. The PM seemed to agree. American audiences, unlike the British, are quite used to a high moral tone being struck by their leaders, I continued. Therefore we need not be afraid of including 'Churchillian' phrases and metaphors, and I said I would coin some to taste. The Americans would love it. In any case, I said, the Churchillian phrases I had in mind would represent MT's true character. They weren't going to be rhetoric – they were going to be herself. (I didn't tell MT, but I must record it here that, running against current chic, I'm an admirer of Churchillian English and have been for a long time. One of the first things I did as head of Radio Free Europe's Third Programme in 1962 was to have Sir Isaiah Berlin's splendid tribute, *Mr Churchill in 1940*, broadcast to Eastern Europe in all the Radio's languages.) Right, she said, and where do we go from there?

I suggested that we should then proceed to saying something about the true meaning of 'revolution' and 'democracy' (a well-flogged argument of mine but always effective), viz. that the only truly new and truly revolutionary force in the world is democracy, not the Soviet system. What we have in the Soviet Union, I said, is as old and depressing as the history of mankind – oppression, the dictatorship of the few, ideological intolerance. This has been the 'normal' thing in human affairs, and the Soviets have cottoned on to that reactionary tradition. Democracy, the tolerance of minority views and interests, freedom of speech and opinion – these are the truly revolutionary phenomena in human affairs. They are still tenuous, even in the Western democracies, and have to be fought for time and again, but they are something we can be proud of. We should make a point of saying so.

The PM, to my surprise, agreed with the idea but not with my vocabulary. 'I don't like the word "revolutionary",' she said, 'and I'm not sure whether I like the word "democracy" either.' I pricked up my ears. 'Why don't we just say', she went on, 'the unprecedented factor in the world is that there is justice, there is law, there is fairness, there is equality before the law and tolerance. These are the new features that distinguish us from Soviet despotism and in fact from most previous forms of government. And from there we can go to the theme I liked so much in your Kirkpatrick piece – that we are the moral conscience of the entire planet.'

The PM's objection to those two words is revealing. It may of course well be that all she had in mind was the violence done to these words in the Soviet vocabulary and the danger of creating confusion in the East, but I rather feel that those were not the true considerations that made her back away from my words. She probably feels that neither democracy nor, most certainly, revolution is a notion we should support without a great many qualifications. If so, I can understand the latter, but her discomfort with 'democracy' worries me. Democracy can be an ass and has frequently been an ass, but it *is* the cornerstone of our thinking and, in our present confrontation with dictatorship, it is a notion we cannot do without. My intention was to use these words precisely because they have been so grievously abused throughout Soviet history. Yet, although I knew she had read her Orwell, I could not quite carry her with me as far as vocabulary was concerned.

The PM liked my various uses of 'myth' when talking about Soviet ideology. We had it in the Kirkpatrick script and I'm going to draft a couple of sentences around it for her transatlantic appearances. In one entry in my *Encounter* piece, Kirkpatrick and I used words to the effect that the intellectual Left in the West has a great capacity for propagating myths of various kinds – the myth that the Soviet Union is ultimately a 'progressive' force, that, for all its shortcomings, it works for the betterment of mankind, and so on. The PM underlined 'myth' in my text. 'It *is* a myth,' she said, 'we must talk about it! We have to name it for what it is. It *is* a myth, damn it. It's time for freedom to take the offensive.'

We then debated what adjective to use to describe the character of the Soviet package of ideological arguments. 'They are false arguments,' she said, 'but it is not quite the word I need. We need something to show that the Soviet case is *wholly* detached from reality and therefore completely misleading. I find the thesaurus mostly inadequate on such occasions. I consult it frequently but seldom hit upon the right word. 'Isn't "spurious" what you are looking for?' I asked. 'That's it, of course, "spurious"; that's the word we want. I want to say something like: we should, in our battle of ideas, puncture every spurious argument and destroy every myth.'

Apropos of 'spurious', Hugh Thomas suggested that we should make a few pointed observations about the scientifically bogus nature of Soviet ideology. The legitimacy of Soviet rule is based on the doctrine of Marxism as interpreted by Lenin. But if one asks what is the evidence that the 1917 October insurrection was indeed an event comparable in its significance to the birth of Jesus Christ or the French Revolution, as Moscow claims, the answer is that Lenin said so. The infallibility on which Soviet communism rests its claim to world leadership is not empirical evidence but revelation. We should, Hugh said, never tire of exposing the fraud that informs the thinking of the Soviet revolution-mongers.

Not only that, I said, but we must also be very careful not to project our own way of thinking and our ethical standards on to the Soviets. They share neither. Yet this is a self-created trap we frequently fall into (Soviet 'parliamentarians'; the Soviet 'judiciary' and so on).

'Ah, but I was happily surprised by the ethical standards and language of some leading Soviet dissidents I had here the other day,' the PM objected. 'They spoke as we did and I believe they think as we do.'

'Westernized dissidents like Bukovsky[1] do', I answered, 'and the more we should respect them for it. But the general mental milieu in the Soviet Union is at odds with ours and will remain so for a long time. Even dissidents like Zinoviev[2] find it difficult to "jump over their shadow", if you will allow a Hungarian metaphor.'

We finally settled for a division of duties between Hugh Thomas and myself. Hugh would tackle the arms control territory, of which I knew virtually nothing, as well as the PM's repeatedly expressed desire that, whatever our differences with the USSR, we must go on talking to their leaders. I would draft the ideological–political message.

I will not give a blow-by-blow account of how the PM took Hugh's and my various suggestions because some will, I hope, be incorporated in her final text. But the bare bones I'm in the process of fleshing out for a speech were roughly these:

---

1. Vladimir Bukovsky, 'Soviet' dissident, former political prisoner, writer.
2. Alexander Zinoviev, Soviet dissident, philosopher and writer.

—The destruction of the Korean airliner was a typical example of the Soviet leadership's contempt for civilized standards and world opinion.

—Advocates in our midst of the 'better red than dead' type of thinking might find themselves ending up both red and dead.

—Vocabulary is all. War and peace are interchangeable notions in Soviet usage. We must not fall into the trap of projecting our own moral standards on to the Soviets. They inhabit a different world.

—In *1984* Orwell prescribes 'two-minute-hate' as a means of attaining ideological rectitude. The Soviets have done better, giving the world sixty-six years of uninterrupted hatred. What does that augur for real peace?

—The Soviet leaders fear the hatred their hatred inspires. But there is no practical evidence that it does. After the Second World War the Americans had a monopoly of nuclear weapons – but made no use of them. Nor did the West punish Soviet aggression in Hungary in 1956 or in Czechoslovakia in 1968. Indeed, while Moscow was imposing satellite status on all of Eastern and Central Europe, Britain and France were dismantling their empires.

—The Soviets have nothing to fear but the poverty, backwardness and subjugation of the peoples under their tutelage.

—Marxist ideology predicts the increasing exploitation and impoverishment of the working class under 'capitalism'. Marx got it wrong. The opposite has happened.

—Soviet ideology holds that we in the West are like rotten apples ready to fall at the first shake of the tree. Some apple, some tree!

—Abroad, the Soviets claim to support the freedom of the ballot box, freedom of speech and the freedom of association. But the USSR itself is run on the principle of one man, one vote – and one candidate.

—Democracies are defensive and peaceful polities. We must always be ready to talk to the Kremlin. Yet we are well advised to keep our powder dry. Trident is an essential part of our defensive capability, and we need Cruise and Pershing missiles on West European soil to maintain the power balance.

—Soviet rhetoric is in many ways even more misleading than was that of Hitler. The Nazi leader made no secret of his plans for conquest and genocide. Moscow, on the other hand, speaks in the name of the liberation of mankind but practises its repression. From Kronstadt to Katyn, the Soviet record is one long indictment of the Kremlin's solemnly given pledges about a radiant and libertarian future.

—What is our answer to Moscow's universal challenge? We accept Andropov's call for a 'struggle for the minds and hearts of billions of people'. The facts of nuclear life have ruled out war, but we can and must fight the battle of ideas. We have the means and much the better case to argue.

—Consider the nature of a functioning modern democracy. It is wholly new, even revolutionary. The Soviet order of things, on the other hand, is entirely in the tradition of despotic princes and intolerant prelates of the Church.

—The Soviet system is therefore a historical throw-back, the great anomaly of our time. Its legitimacy rests on revelation – not reason. In this, too, it is a fitting successor to the world's traditional despotisms.

—Freedom and prosperity are two sides of the same coin. So are tyranny and poverty.

—Where is the sting of communism in a free competition of ideas and achievements? We support Reagan's 'democracy project' as outlined at Windsor Castle.

—But caution is in order. Competing with the Soviets with all peaceful means at our disposal cannot mean *détente* as Moscow understands it. The Aesopian fable of the sun and the wind still stands.

—Our public opinion must understand that *détente* for the Soviet leaders means the continuation of the Cold War with other means. In fairness to them: they have never sought to hide this from us. That we have chosen to be deceived tells us something about Western governments, the psychology of the 1970s and the skill of Soviet subversion and propaganda.

—We have become the 'universal uncles' of the entire world, including the communist world. We think and build and care not only for ourselves, but also for the well-being of the whole of mankind. In a world in which there is much darkness and poverty, Western societies have become the iron-reserve of the physical needs of the entire planet and the repository of its conscience.

—We rejoice in this legacy. It is a challenge of which only free and responsible men and women are capable of becoming aware, and to which they alone can do justice. It is a challenge Winston Churchill would have understood and welcomed.

Around 4 p.m. the PM had an appointment with her eye specialist. Excusing herself she said: 'Would the two of you like to make a start while I'm seeing my doctor? I should be back in a couple of hours.' But Hugh and I were exhausted. Neither of us had any experience of speech-writing on the hoof. We said we'd rather do it at our leisure and promised to let her have a coordinated draft early next week. So ended a memorable Saturday.

20 September 1983

Swapped ideas with Hugh Thomas on the phone. He repeated what he had told me after our day with the PM at Chequers: 'You are now being drawn into the prime minister's circle. But don't be upset or disappointed if she does not make full use of the advice you've given or the texts you have supplied. Awful things can happen. Sometimes the PM will use only parts of your work or none. She may recast it or combine it with some Foreign Office draft. One must not feel sensitive about this.'

Spoke to Charlie Douglas-Home on the phone. He had similar advice to offer. Working with MT is a labour of love, he said; don't feel you've wasted your time if your contribution is not being used or not being used the way you think it ought to be.

Well, I'm unlikely to feel either upset or disappointed. I am in fact very pleased to have been asked to help in the first place. If my brainchild is to be an orphan, I'll have proof of it soon enough.

21 September 1983

Finished draft and took it up to Hugh Thomas in London. He gave me his, mainly on arms control. The two will now be put together and given to the PM. Hugh's text is more down to earth than mine – which is probably as well. It is a closely argued brief for talks with the Soviets but from a position of strength and preserving a sense of 'ruthless realism'. He reminds us under his fourth point that Lenin in 1917 recalled with satisfaction the dictum of Clausewitz that the most successful conqueror is one who captures a city by intimidation, without a shot fired. Any government known to have killed thousands of its own army officers and hundreds of thousands of the ruling party members is naturally something to fear if it threatens a neighbour, he says. Some of his points slightly overlap with mine, but he has crafted a very incisive and practical argument. A splendid political understanding and a warm personal friendship have arisen between Hugh and myself over the last two or so years. I value it enormously. Hugh's impressive learning, charm and wit are in stark contrast with the base metal in the political world.

30 September–3 October 1983

Judging from the text published in *The Times*, MT seems to have used a great deal of my draft. No doubt I'll get copy when the lady is back. What I heard on radio and television on Thursday (29th) and Friday was gratifying, if only because the speech made Dennis Healey[1] mad. He called her 'an ignorant and opinionated demagogue' who was deliberately trying to torpedo the nuclear arms talks. A BBC commentator noted from Washington: 'In Toronto and last night here, she seemed to be embarked on some kind of an anti-

---

1. Later Lord Healey of Riddlesden; former deputy leader of the Labour Party; former chancellor of the exchequer.

communist crusade, using deliberately Churchillian rhetoric.' I felt thrilled to see the PM on television uttering some of my thoughts and phrases.

Waiting for the print media reactions on Friday and Saturday, two things happened. I was rung by Jim Buckley[1] from Munich and offered the Radio Free Europe directorship, which I accepted subject to certain conditions – but I'm not completely convinced that I've done the right thing. Munich will be challenging, but it will cut me off from my friends in this country. I told Hugh Thomas over the phone about the coming appointment. He was glad to hear it and said he would inform the PM. He thought she too would be supportive because she felt it was important that people of our kind of mentality should be in charge of the principal communications channels *vis-à-vis* the Soviets.

The second thing of note was a long chat I had on the phone with Jeane Kirkpatrick. She had been at the Churchill Award dinner and was full of enthusiasm. It was a glittering occasion, she said, the PM made a fighting speech. She sounded Churchillian, she read her words wonderfully, and so on. Then she asked jokingly: 'And you wrote it, didn't you?' 'My lips are sealed,' I said. 'Well,' she answered, 'I know what I know. Margaret Thatcher sought me out at the dinner and said "Talking to Charlie Douglas-Home the other day I heard from him that you and George Urban have recorded a marvellous conversation which Charlie will shortly publish. In George Urban we have a common friend".' Apparently MT did not disclose that she had herself seen the text or that we had made use of it at Chequers. So, not to underbid the PM, I said nothing.

MT's general reception in America is euphoric. Reagan sent her a magnificent tribute to mark the Churchill Award: 'World affairs today demand the boldness and integrity of a Churchill. In his absence, I know he would want us to look to you as the legendary Britannia, a special lady, the greatest defender of the realm.'

---

1. James L. Buckley, president of Radio Free Europe/Radio Liberty; former US senator.

Here, we have wide and mostly positive media coverage:

The Times leads with a front-page report under 'Thatcher delivers blistering attack on Soviet tyranny', and also carries a near-complete text of the speech under 'Thatcher denounces Kremlin in fiery Washington speech'. There is also a very substantial and highly supportive first leader in the Saturday paper ('Answering Back'), written probably by Charlie. It is no less emphatic than the speech itself.

The *Guardian*'s headline is 'Thatcher gets tough on missiles'. The Canadian speech, it says 'was tough even by her own "Iron Lady" standards'. But the Washington speech was clearly too much for the paper. 'Thatcher fuels the cold war of words', is its front-page headline. In a leader it says: 'It is not simply that the Iron Lady is unflinching in the fray: she seems almost to glory in its challenges. There is not just Churchill in her rhetoric: there is Harry before Agincourt, even Richard the Lionheart, setting out for the Holy War with Saladin ... But once you begin to talk about your antagonist in the language of the third crusade it becomes difficult ever to escape from it.'

The *Daily Telegraph* says: 'Thatcher spurs West to win battle of ideas'.

The *Mail* has a supportive leader: 'Mrs Thatcher tells it the way it is. ... there is no doubt that ... in this latest visit of hers to America, Mrs Thatcher has been a great hit ... Her strength all along has been that she says what she believes, not merely what is popular with the public or the media élite. Her American audience – like the British electorate – recognise this.'

Unsurprisingly, the *Mirror* is down on us. Under 'Old Men Forget', it says: 'Mr Reagan, now in the flower of his old age, denounces Mr Andropov while Mrs Thatcher enthusiastically plays Little Miss Echo. Mr Andropov, insecure and unhealthy, denounces back. They are two Cold War veterans, old men who live in the past and forget the future.'

The *Express* is predictably exuberant. Under the title of 'Hard-headed Maggie's new double act', it says: 'When it comes to being tough, Mrs Thatcher is now way ahead of all-comers. Her Washington speech, labelling the Soviets as "a modern version of the early tyrannies of history", makes her admiring host President Reagan look like a latter-day Peacenik.'

The *Sun* too is robust in its usual, intellectually undemanding way. 'Be Strong' is its editorial headline, followed by: 'The appeasers are at it again, urging Margaret Thatcher not to be beastly to the Russians. "The choice is between negotiation and incineration", declares one whining voice. Not so, the choice is between strength and incineration. The Soviet leaders must be left in no doubt of Britain's determination to defend herself.'

3 October 1983

Had Hugh Thomas on the phone. We discussed the Sunday press, which leaves a lot to be desired. Julian Critchley has put his knife into MT on general grounds, unrelated to the speeches. A very ugly attack. The *Sunday Times* has a splendid American tour-description by Michael Jones, and in the *Sunday Telegraph* Alexander Chancellor produces a typically wet argument: 'If Mr Reagan and Mrs Thatcher are right, if the Russians are just marauding beasts devoid of any moral constraints, it clearly would be pointless to negotiate with them ... Unless it is war they want, the Prime Minister and the President should ask themselves if it is wise to abuse the Russians so intemperately ... Mr Reagan and Mrs Thatcher simply make their own peace overtures appear futile.' This is balanced, however, by the *Telegraph*'s leader: 'Pressures upon public opinion to promote passivity in the West are far stronger than those promoting belligerency. Wishful thinking about the Soviet Union springs eternal in the liberal heart, and there is no shortage of persuasive voices counselling the soft approach. Plain speaking still has the capacity to shock, which is precisely why it is still so necessary.'

Hugh asked whether I was aware that some people in the US press had described the PM's Churchill speech as another Fulton address? I wasn't, but it is flattering.

Around 7 p.m. last night, while I was talking on the phone to a friend in Germany, Pat burst in: 'Hang up quickly, the prime minister is on the other line.'

Here was news. I had not heard from her since Chequers. I could hardly suppress my excitement. A Downing Street operator handed me to the lady. 'Margaret Thatcher speaking,' she said very formally but with a warm tone in her voice. And we were to spend the next half-hour on the telephone in what amounted to a mutually morale-boosting survey of the events of the last few days. The PM was in overdrive. The American trip had been a triumph. She wanted to share her excitement and sample mine in return. I was glad to be given a chance to convey it.

'I want to thank you very much for the wonderful help you've given me with my American speech,' she said. 'I'm sure you realize that I used a great deal of your text, and even those parts I was not able to fit in I've stowed away in my mind. And some of the quotations you gave me from Lenin I'll certainly use in Parliament and elsewhere.'

She then asked how the media had played her speeches and whether I had seen her on the box or heard her on radio. I assured her that I had done little else over the last three days, and that the reaction here was on the whole very good though unsurprising; her supporters supported, her opponents opposed, though some of the first wobbled. She had already heard about Dennis Healey's abusive words.

'Do you think he has actually read the speech? I doubt it. Physically he couldn't have done so as he said what he did first thing Friday morning – much before the text was released. Isn't that typical of Healey? Do you remember what he said about me during the election campaign?'

'I do indeed,' I said, 'and I should think it was Healey's attack that won you the election.'

'He certainly helped us a great deal. The British public hate unfairness; they have an uncanny sense for pinpointing it.'

What the PM was referring to was a poisonous 'Healeyism' which would have earned him a challenge to a duel in an earlier age. In the (1983) election campaign he said in a speech in Birmingham that Margaret Thatcher had been 'glorying in slaughter' during the Falklands war. 'She wrapped herself in the Union Jack and exploited the sacrifices of servicemen during the Falklands conflict for party advantage, while lending money to Buenos Aires so that the Argentines could buy more weapons to kill more British servicemen.' Healey had to apologize, but he did so ambiguously. The June election was in the bag, in my estimation, long before Healey made his ill-judged comment (Neil Kinnock[1] was being no fairer), but he helped to ensure that Conservative victory at the polls was decisive.

MT then quoted various passages from the speech to stress the bits she liked most and thought she had deployed to best effect. Several appeared to have come from my stable. 'As I was reading the speech,' she said, 'I was very conscious of the concentrated attention I was receiving. You could hear a pin drop. It was a marvellous occasion. I thought my delivery was rather good and so were the acoustics of the room. I didn't have to raise my voice too much. How did it come over on television?'

I assured her that there had been ample, though for me insufficient, coverage, that she had been shown in a number of close-ups, that the cameras had picked up George Shultz[2], Jeane Kirkpatrick and other notables sitting in the audience, and of course the award-giving ceremony culminating in Reagan's tribute.

'Yes, Jeane Kirkpatrick was there. I spoke to her and we made things up.'

'Do you mean your tiff about the Falklands issue?'

'Yes; I didn't mention the Falklands, but I chatted to her at some length and praised her work.'

'I understand you may be moving to Munich,' the PM went on. 'Tell me about Radio Free Europe. What exactly does it do, who controls it, who pays for it?' I gave her a short description and said

---

1. Leader of the Labour Party 1983–92.
2. United States secretary of state, 1982–89.

that although I'd be in Munich for perhaps three years, I would go on being active at the Centre for Policy Studies.

She came back to the speech. 'Those Lenin quotations you gave me are most important. They are brutal to a degree. That is why it is so important not to think that your enemy shares your own assumptions about what is right and what is wrong in public life, or in private life for that matter. I'm glad we made such a point of the danger of projecting our own morality on to the other side. That was the most important thing I said in Washington.'

'It is very hard to get Western journalists to understand', I said, 'that the very language they write in and the very spectacles they wear when looking at the Soviet world carry a distorting factor much to the disadvantage of independent judgement. They hate being reminded of this because the imaginative leap from our civilization to that of the communist world is too difficult.'

'Yes,' she said, 'and in addition to that we have a large number of people in all Western countries who are gripped by an entirely false sense of Soviet power, the menace it represents to our world, the true motivations of the Soviet leaders, the character of Soviet Man, and so on. Some believe what they do quite sincerely, but others are so bent on hating the Right that they lull themselves into a state of mental appeasement on the 'anything to annoy this lot' principle. That is why we have to say the things we said in Washington and Ottawa again and again.'

'Repetition is unfortunately of the essence,' I said, 'even though those of us who do the repeating often can't bear to hear our own arguments recycled now in this, now in that form. But it has to be done: the general public is on the whole disinterested, its attention span is short, and its historical memory minimal – factors that do not sit well with our praise of democracy.'

'Incidentally, Prime Minister,' I said, 'Hugh Thomas and I were thinking of hammering Dennis Healey for his words. We thought we might persuade Hugh Seton-Watson[1] or someone else of his stature

---

1. Professor of Russian history, London University.

to write to *The Times*: which of these points in Mrs Thatcher's speech does Mr Healey disagree with? That the Soviet Union is a dictatorship? That it is trying to bring communism to the entire world? That it has taken the whole of Eastern and Central Europe by force or the threat of force? That it is a renewed threat to its 'fraternal' neighbours under the 'Brezhnev Doctrine'? That it has slaughtered millions of its own people under Stalin and is still intolerant of any form of dissent – especially social democracy? We thought Healey would find it a little difficult to disagree with these propositions, especially as he had himself subscribed to them at various times in his very honourable, post-communist career.'

The PM said, yes, it would be a blow for truth to puncture Healey's assertions. They *are* absurd.

In parting she asked whether I could send her some ideas for her Party Conference speech and then for the Lord Mayor's dinner in the Guildhall.

'One other thing,' she said. 'I incorporated in my Washington speech your nice passage about the Hungarian poet – was his name Pilinszky? You used it in the Kirkpatrick article but did not put it into my draft. I thought it was so telling an illustration of what we were saying about the West being the conscience of the planet that I used it: "You in the West", said an Hungarian poet, "have a special duty because you are free. That freedom is both a blessing and a burden, for it makes you spiritually responsible for the whole of humanity." I hope that was alright with you.'

Indeed it was.

5 October 1983

A large brown government envelope arrived yesterday. In it: a warm thank-you letter from the prime minister with copies of her two speeches. The latter are marked for emphasis in her hand.

'You will see', she wrote, 'that I drew heavily on your most helpful contributions, especially for the Winston Churchill speech. It will interest you that Jeane Kirkpatrick was present at the Washington dinner and indeed shared a table with me.'

12 October 1983

This should be my last entry about the speech-writing episode. Hugh and I made no disclosure and provided no indication as to the identity of the speech writers, yet on 10 October we were named by Peter Stothard[1] in *The Times*:

> The Prime Minister is in high spirits after her trip to North America. She considers her three speeches there among the best she has ever made. The fiercely anti-Soviet line emerged from a seminar at Chequers attended by Lord (Hugh) Thomas, Mr George Urban (the Sovietologist whose conversation with Jeane Kirkpatrick is being published in *The Times* this week) and her Foreign Office private secretary, John Coles, vainly representing his master's more cautious voices.

Hugh is upset because he thinks the PM might be. He suspects Stothard's information must have come from Charlie. I share that; but does it really matter? Let's hope the lady doesn't explode.

The only other mentioning of names (mine, as it happened) came five days later from Colin Welch in the *Spectator*. Colin is an *Encounter* colleague, a man of sophisticated wit and vast knowledge, especially in the Germanic field. 'As for stridency,' he wrote,

> it has come to a pretty pass, when the sober expression of the most undeniable truths about Russia (based, I understand, on advice from Mr George Urban, who knows Russia better than Mrs Thatcher's critics know their way up the back stairs) can be so characterised – a measure of our decline into equivocation, dependency and sycophancy, of our self-Finlandisation.

At the Labour Party Conference Michael Foot, the outgoing leader, accused MT of having 'given an astonishing and amazing

---

1. Features editor, later editor, of *The Times*.

performance' during her recent visit to the United States. Britain should have offered cool advice instead of throwing faggots onto the flames. If Mrs Thatcher's rhetoric were turned into action there would be no possibility of agreement on arms control. He said he was against the deployment of Cruise and Pershing missiles. Nothing unexpected there.

But the most curious criticisms have come from the Tory side. Enoch Powell[1] feels the American view of the USSR as a hostile and expanionist power is self-serving and all wrong. Mrs Thatcher has been caught up in that false view of history, he writes in the *Guardian*.

> I refer to the misunderstanding of Soviet Russia as an aggressive power, militaristically and ideologically bent upon world domina-tion – 'seeing', to quote a recent speech of the British Prime Minister, 'the rest of the world as its rightful fiefdom'. How any rational person, viewing objectively the history of the last thirty-five years, could entertain this 'international misunderstanding' challenges, if it does not defeat, comprehension. The notion has no basis in fact ... If Russia is bent on world conquest, she has been remarkably slothful and remarkably unsuccessful.

Abrupt changes in Enoch Powell's views have become so customary (I first knew him as a fervent pro-European) that I no longer take him seriously.

Even more curious is Lord Gladwyn's letter in *The Times* – very much the letter of a former diplomat –

> negotiations on arms control and limitation are the only way in which ... the danger of war can be notably reduced, if not elimin-ated ... But if you are to negotiate – and are even condemned to succeed – it hardly helps if, whatever your feelings, you say openly that you regard your partner as an enemy of the human race.

Even George Walden[2] – a man I greatly like and respect, and now

---

1. Conservative thinker, former Conservative minister of health.
2. Conservative MP.

a Conservative MP – cannot resist some inspired carping. He writes in *The Times* (5 October 1983),

> We cannot and should not try to shout down the Russians. That will not make them go away, and they will always win the contest of abuse … In her speech in Washington last week, the Prime Minister rightly drew attention to the superiority of Western culture. 'Culture hates hatred', said Matthew Arnold. So, I suspect, do the British. We shall not keep public opinion with us if East–West exchanges continue at their present pitch. There will be a reaction. All sorts of people – not just the weak and the wobbly – will start to shrink back, and to ask whether we have got the nuclear arithmetic right … some will be tempted to find excuses for the Russians in their anxiety to 'correct the balance'.

David Watt,[1] a wet, also writing in *The Times* (7 October 1983) has gone one better:

> Margaret Thatcher's extraordinary outburst against the Soviet Union in Washington last week has attracted enough criticism to keep her happy for weeks … There is no point in wasting time on the … calculation Mrs. Thatcher is supposed to have made: that tough talking by the British Prime Minister will have some practical effect on Soviet behaviour. It is so absurd that I do not believe that the Prime Minister really entertains it herself … She sees herself in the wrong heroic context. The wretched analogy with the 1930s and the appeasement of Hitler has in varying contexts misled generation after generation of politicians … Mrs Thatcher has no need of posturings and nor do we. War is not inevitable because we have deterred it. What we need now, perhaps, as Churchill might have said, is more jaw-jaw.

The *Sun* (alas, the disgusting *Sun* of all papers! – I almost hesitate to quote it but will do as it speaks the truth) has unkind things to say about Francis Pym:

> Isn't Francis Pym priceless? The ex-Foreign Secretary goes on

---

1. Journalist, director of the Royal Institute of International Affairs, 1978–83.

the radio to attack Margaret Thatcher for denouncing Russian tyranny. But then he adds that what she said was 'undoubtedly true'. In that case, why ever shouldn't she say it? One of the besetting sins of our diplomats is that they shrink from telling the Soviet Union and other hostile countries exactly what they think ... Master Pym is by no means the only doubletalk specialist who should have been booted out of the Foreign Office!

6 November 1983

This really must be my last entry about the Churchill speech. I cannot resist quoting, in conclusion, my old friend Bob Conquest[1] (from yesterday's *Daily Telegraph*), partly because he was there in Washington to hear MT's speech, and partly because I'd be hard put to it to answer our Conservative critics more cogently than he does.

Mrs Thatcher's recent Washington Embassy speech ... produced a notable outpour of drivel – needless to say from Conservative 'wets' as well as others. Her remarks (I was present and heard them) were clearly and firmly expressed, and absolutely true. Clear and firm expression is denounced as 'rhetoric' and truth thought better unsaid. One Tory superwet, or megawet, even argued, first that though the Russians abuse us we should never answer back, and that if we both attacked each other verbally this would prevent negotiations. Of course this equates Mrs Thatcher's true remarks with their false ones; and the Kremlin will negotiate if it feels it to be in its interests whatever our speeches, as it happily did with a far more abusive Hitler. More important, we can only negotiate realistically, if we know our adversary, and if our leaders transmit that knowledge to the public.

1. Robert Conquest, poet and historian of Soviet and Russian affairs.

CHAPTER 3

At the Peak of her Fame

The annual general meetings of the Centre for Policy Studies were more than reviews of the Centre's yearly activities – they tended to be re-dedications to the Thatcherite creed, with Margaret Thatcher personally officiating as inspiration and celebrant. Yet it would be misleading to think of them as gatherings of the Conservative Right only. In the early 1980s, the Conservative Party was a broad church, largely at peace with itself in the wake of the Falklands war, and enjoying an almost un-hindered exercise of power. The bugbear of European integration had not yet begun to divide the Party, and the miners' insurrection was a prospect many Tories, though not Margaret Thatcher, thought could be wished away.

Diary

31 January 1984

Yesterday, I spoke at the Centre's annual general meeting on behalf of our Soviet study group. It was my first experience of sharing a platform with the PM.

A few weeks ago, Hugh Thomas contacted me in Munich wonder-ing whether I would take on two 'small' assignments: assist the PM with ideas for her forthcoming visit to Hungary – themes for speeches and the like – and speak about Soviet–Eastern European policy on behalf of our group at the AGM on 30 January. I readily agreed to both, recalling the PM's stirring addresses at earlier AGMs and the insight these gatherings offered into the mentality of the

Conservative establishment. I've been close to but never really part of this establishment, so I was keen to fill in the gaps in my experience. MT was a marvel of enthusiasm and practical good sense on these occasions, with a fine gift for putting her ideas in succinct and print-ready sentences. Because of her presence, we always drew the cream of the intellectual–spiritual element in the Conservative Party, tangling with whom was stimulating and frequently pleasurable.

As to the Hungarian assignment – I was happy to take it on and set to work at once. An essay on Anglo-Hungarian relations in the nineteenth century had won me a visiting fellowship many years ago. I could build on that and on decades of having gone native in this country as a naturalized Briton. But Hugh's vague brief, which seemed uncontroversial enough early in October, became a bit of a headache by the end of the month.

The American intervention in Grenada and the PM's strong reaction to it began to affect Anglo-American and Anglo-Soviet relations. She was and still is profoundly upset by the violation (as she sees it) of Commonwealth sovereignty, and let it be known in private that this might be a good time to reassess our relations with Moscow. I see this volte-face (if that is what it will turn out to be) more as pique than as an expression of a considered policy and I don't think it will last, but while it does we'll have to bear it in mind.

Hugh Thomas, who is much more closely involved with her than I am, feels the same. On 15 December he wrote to me: 'Could we have a word about your speech for January 30? I think, for good or evil, the Prime Minister is toying with the idea of some kind of an approach to the USSR – so she does not want to be undercut, as it were, by us saying such things more fully. Also she has not yet come out of the fury with the US over Grenada and that needs to be considered.'

What this meant was that Hugh, remembering my strong anti-Soviet commitment and how it had been articulated in the PM's Churchill Award speech, was just a little apprehensive that I might say things at the AGM that would undoubtedly reach Soviet ears and prejudice the PM's freedom of manoeuvre if, indeed, there was to be a 'new approach' to the Kremlin in the wake of Grenada.

I immediately phoned Hugh. I could well see a case for my standing down, I said, for I might indeed say things that would not fit in with the PM's new thinking, especially as we didn't know what the new thinking was. On Hungary, too, I wouldn't be upset in the slightest if on second thoughts I were considered too *parti pris* to equip her with ideas.

Hugh, however, wouldn't have any of that. He insisted that I should go ahead with both and that we'd put our heads together if problems arose. So I wrote my speech trying hard to sound reasonable; but I couldn't, of course, betray the truth as I saw it, or my principles. I said, for example: 'The Soviets' notion of peaceful coexistence incorporates the notion of warlike coexistence' – not a very strong thing to say but hurtful to Soviet ears. And later: 'The peoples of Eastern Europe are our allies. They constitute, in a paradoxical manner, the "Communist encirclement" of the Soviet Union.' If the PM was serious about making friendlier noises to the Soviet Union, these sentences would certainly not help. But – this was *my* speech, and I was determined to accept only very minor alterations in tone and none in substance. The former came a few days later in the shape of tentative suggestions from the PM herself – to which I'll return presently.

Hugh Thomas, like me, took a poor view of any 'new', i.e. softer, approach being made to the USSR on the rebound from Grenada. Indeed, he thought the PM had failed to understand the aggressive character of Soviet–Cuban policy in the Caribbean and the fears it was inspiring in Washington. Late in October, while I was in London on the Radio's business, Hugh invited me to the Lords' debate on Grenada (1 November) in which he was going to make a speech and, as I now know, break ranks with the government. He was not the only Conservative to do so. The dissenters included the Lords Home, Greenhill, Annan, Beloff, Soames and others. Less surprisingly, some (though not all) Labour peers, too, were critical, and a good deal of wit was harnessed to riding old hobby-horses against the Reaganite Right. Wayland Young (Lord Kennet) and Roy Jenkins (Lord Jenkins) were on particularly good form, supporting in effect the government's critique of the American violation of Commonwealth sovereignty but doing it with so destructive a purpose that the government was more likely to be deeply embarrassed than grateful. Roy Jenkins, having announced that President Reagan's 'grasp of his marbles sometimes seems to be precarious', charged that the government's reliance on American crews to safeguard Britain's security was an act of madness. One sentence, wholly unjustified in substance but delicious for its insolence, struck me as a gem: 'If the government will not learn the lesson of Grenada and are determined to allow the Americans to have operational control over cruise missiles, then we should all get a copy of the Voluntary Euthanasia Society's booklet on safe methods of suicide and leave this earth at a time of our own choosing rather than leave it to President Reagan to decide when we go.'

All this was scintillating and huge fun – so much so that next day I rang Mel Lasky[1] urging him to reproduce extracts from Hansard – which he has now done with his usual editorial brilliance (*Encounter*, January 1984). Hugh's own dissent was straightforward: 'It is my considered belief', he said, 'that the United States was justified in the action which it took.' The PM won't like this.

I was especially intrigued by Lord Gladwyn's rather more cautious contribution, for he spoke about Grenada only indirectly, concentrating his fire on Reagan's foreign policy as (allegedly) represented by my long dialogue with Jeane Kirkpatrick in the November 1983 issue of *Encounter* magazine:

We are discovering, rather belatedly, that the American Administration has a very different idea of how best to conduct the continuing struggle with a vast totalitarian superpower (which is commonly and accurately known as the Cold War) from that which until now, broadly speaking, has been accepted by the other members of the North Atlantic Alliance.

1. Melvin J. Lasky, principal editor of the monthly journal *Encounter*.

The point is well brought out by a long and absorbing dialogue in the latest number of the magazine *Encounter*, between George Urban, an intellectual standing slightly to the Right of Solzhenitsyn, and Jeane Kirkpatrick, the highly intelligent, if not uncontroversial, American representative on the United Nations Security Council, who probably knows more about the Cold War than most.

From this long dialogue, which I urge noble Lords to read if they are interested in the subject, we gather that the West must abandon all idea of, as it were, 'taming' the Soviet regime; that is to say, by so operating *détente* as to achieve a sort of 'Westernising' of the Soviet Union with which a deal might eventually be made. On the contrary, all means short of an actual fighting war should be employed in order to weaken the Soviet regime, and nothing whatever should be done to strengthen it, this principle applying more especially, of course, to economic assistance. Naturally, too, all spontaneous resistance to Soviet domination, whether in the Union itself or in the satellites, should be actively encouraged, though not to the point of actually offering military help.

It follows that, short of provoking war – and on this point Jeane Kirkpatrick is, happily, most insistent – all possible measures designed to weaken the Soviet Union and its satellites should be taken, more especially – and this is the point – in Central and South America where any frankly pro-Soviet regimes must, if possible, be, as it were, immunised or at least rendered incapable of harming the United States in what must be regarded by the Europeans as an American sphere of interest. It is also argued that, while 'democratic' regimes are by far the best, 'authoritarian' Governments may well have to be tolerated, seeing that, however repressive, they are at least far preferable to 'totalitarian' ones.

Well, if this is the general policy of the Reagan Administration, and there is much evidence to show that it is, what are the European members of the North Atlantic Treaty going to do about it?

I was surprised by Gladwyn's surprise and wrote to Hugh to say so. But, horror of horrors, Gladwyn is Hugh's father-in-law! What a *faux pas*! Hugh, however, was quite wonderful about it. 'Lord Gladwyn, as you may know, is my father-in-law,' he wrote on 14

November. 'I think he was in an extremely complicated position during that debate since I believe he really sided with us but felt he had to express the Liberal view. His other remarks are very odd, I quite agree, and I have taken this up with him.'

Ignorance never pays, but I have an unworldly way of not wanting to know about the family connections and personal lives of my friends – an intellectual aloofness of sorts which tends to cause me from time to time quite a bit of embarrassment. I have always found the presence of wives, husbands and other relations an obstacle to any serious talk, and my abhorrence of parties is well known. Hence I'm seldom invited – for which the Lord be praised.

Yesterday our study group met for lunch (Hugh Thomas, Hugh Seton-Watson, Dominic Lieven[1], Malcolm Macintosh[2] and I) at the CPS as a prelude to the AGM in the evening. The PM's visit to Hungary was very much on our minds. I had drafted a number of themes for her, stressing various familiar connecting tissues in the two countries' history: Magna Carta and the Golden Bull; Kossuth's reception in England and Scotland; and the coincidence of British and Hungarian interests and sentiments under present conditions.

We were trying to decide whom the visit would benefit most: would it underline MT's incipient Gaullism *vis-à-vis* the Americans, weakening the cohesion of the West? That would be buying British 'independence' at a ruinous price. Could her praise of the liberal-izing elements in the Kádár economy and in Hungarian culture assist the reformers without making life unduly difficult for Kádár in Moscow? Excessive public approval of Hungary's liberal ways by a person like MT is much feared in Budapest. No approval, on the other hand, and no visible differentiation from hardline governments such as the Romanian, Czechoslovak and East German, would be taken amiss and reduce British influence.

We decided that a cautious halfway house was the answer. Our

1. Lecturer, later professor, of Russian history at the London School of Economics.
2. Military historian, member of the Cabinet Office.

fear that the visit might provide a launching pad for an Anglo-Gaullism of sorts was limited because differentiation – rewarding the more liberal communists while keeping aloof from the fully repressive ones – has been American policy, too, for a long time, even though it has not always been properly implemented. Ceauşescu[1] and his terrible gang have been indulged, even supported, by the State Department because they are thought to be a thorn in the flesh of Moscow. Some thorn! I'm told by Dick Perle[2] that Ceauşescu is one of the Kremlin's secret conduits for the transfer of high-technology equipment banned under Cocom.[3]

After lunch Hugh Thomas returned my text for the evening's speech. He had shown it to the PM and she had pencilled in two small cuts subject to what I thought. I looked at these with great interest but, to my disappointment, both were probably cuts for modesty only. In the first case, my text said: 'They [the Soviet leaders] tended to get it wrong more often than right. For example, their recent assessment of how much "peace" propaganda the West German public would assimilate on the eve of missile deployment to prevent deployment, proved false. So did their hope at the time of the Falklands conflict that British public opinion would disown the policies of the Government and the Government itself lose its nerve. Marx and Lenin proved poor guides to the nerve of the Prime Minister.' The last sentence was queried by the PM. She probably thought it was in questionable taste. I cut it out, though true it certainly was.

In the second case, my text said: 'We might do worse than pit a "Thatcher-doctrine" against the one associated with the name of Mr Brezhnev, stressing our solidarity with the peaceful aspirations of the nations of Eastern Europe and offering cooperation to those of their governments that render themselves accountable, or more accountable, to the wishes of the people.' Here she had pencilled in

---

1. Nicolai Ceauşescu, Romanian president, 1974–89.
2. United States assistant secretary of state for security policy, 1981–87.
3. Coordinating Committee for Multilateral Export Control.

the opening clause for a cut. I accepted this without demur. My meaning was clear enough without the Thatcher–Brezhnev contrast. The revised sentence simply read: 'We should stress our solidarity with the peaceful aspirations of the nations of Eastern Europe,' etc.

My speech did take into account the PM's forthcoming visit to Hungary and was marginally 'milder' than it might otherwise have been. But I said nothing I do not profoundly believe in: some of the satellites *are* rapidly distancing themselves from Moscow; communism *is* losing its grip everywhere; the magnetism of Europe *is* paramount throughout the Soviet glacis; the Ukrainians, Uzbeks and Tatars *do* want to carve out separate national lives for themselves, and even in Russia democratic traditions, thin as they are, are slowly reasserting themselves. On all these we can cautiously build provided we remain strong and relentlessly tough with the Kremlin.

But not everyone in the audience was satisfied. When the meeting was over, Alfred Sherman[1], that not very pleasant, self-appointed founding-father of Thatcherism, came up to me to chide me. 'You were too soft on the Soviets,' he said. Foolishly, I let myself in for an explanation. With MT's visit to Hungary only a few days away, I said, one had to bear in mind what she could be reasonably expected to embrace as government policy. But that wouldn't pacify Sherman. 'Well,' he observed rather grandly, 'self-censorship is not a thing I approve of. I left the Communist Party because I wouldn't allow it. They tried to interfere with my thinking, but I wouldn't have it.'

'I fail to see a parallel,' I said, 'and you shouldn't have been a communist in the first place, much less a member of the Communist Party.' How MT got herself so thoroughly mixed up with this very clever but twisted man is still a mystery to me. Keith Joseph's help is not enough to explain it. Sherman once called on us for tea in

---

1. Later, Sir Alfred Sherman, journalist and writer, formerly director of studies, Centre for Policy Studies. In the Bosnian war he served as policy adviser of the self-styled Serbian government in Pale under Radovan Karadžić and General Ratko Mladić – both indicted, in 1995, for suspected war crimes by the United Nations War Crimes Tribunal.

Brighton. My wife swore she would never allow him to cross our threshhold again.

I'll spend little time on the AGM itself, for much of it was routine. Hugh Thomas provided the usual panegyric to the PM and our donors, but he did so most elegantly and with a fine sense of humour. The Bohemian in Hugh surfaces even when he makes formal speeches. I love that trait in him. Is there some subliminal Celtic–Hungarian affinity at work here? Early in his chairmanship of the Centre, Hugh invited me to join him 'cold' – purely on the strength of my published work. We had never met.

Hugh Seton-Watson, who spoke before me, made a number of important points which may have left some of our more sanguine listeners (certainly Sherman) dissatisfied. Soviet reality, he said, had to be looked at at different levels and from different points of view. This, he said, is difficult for the Western democratic mind, which likes to think in terms of either/or. For example, Third World crises are not caused either by local conditions or by Soviet-sponsored subversion, but usually by both. Western democracies don't have a choice of either maintaining their defences or negotiating with the USSR: they have to do both. This was a hint at the naïve American perception of *détente* that claimed Kissinger among its victims.

Hugh was particularly good on ideology – always a difficult problem to grasp for untheological Englishmen. His message was: don't underestimate the importance of the ideological element in Soviet policy-making. For us, the recital of the incantations of Marxism-Leninism may be ridiculous, but it would be wrong to think that the Soviet leaders do not believe it. For them, their own lives, and even more the growth of the Soviet Union in their lifetime, are a tremendous success story; and this success has been achieved 'under the banner of Marxism-Leninism'. The legitimacy of the whole regime depends on this policy. Its exclusive wisdom has been handed down to them from Lenin to successive generations of appointed members of the Central Committee and the secretary-general. From this ideology derives their mission to lead the human race to the inevitable culmination of history, the universal triumph of socialism.

And we must be clear that socialism for them means the Soviet system. No other system is socialism by definition. Hugh's words went down extremely well. He sounds and looks like a man of profound wisdom – which he certainly is.

My own speech, too, was well received. My delivery was adequate – no more. I thought the audience was listening with considerable attention, as Hugh Seton-Watson's and my contributions probably represented the business-end of the evening's proceedings in foreign affairs, apart, of course, from the PM's. But while Hugh spoke in general terms about our relations with Moscow, my remarks were in some ways an unofficial indication of how the PM might tackle Hungary and the other Eastern/Central Europeans in the coming months. I got a good applause. As soon as I had finished, Hugh Thomas, reaching behind the PM's back, handed me a pencilled note: 'Dear George, you did very well indeed. Thank you. You were listened to with rapt attention by people who may not have thought about these issues.' He was most generous – he always is.

Then it was our founder's turn to address the faithful. The PM was magnificent. She had made only the flimsiest of notes while the rest of us were speaking, yet she was highly organized, fluent and persuasive. With two famous election victories behind her, she is brimming with self-confidence. Her message was the usual: restoring the balance of power between the state and the citizen, reducing direct taxation, creating rather than distributing wealth and constraining public expenditure. She was radical about personal capital formation: 'every man, a man of property; every man with a bit of his own', warning, however, that the language on this had to be got right, for 'personal capital formation will not win a lot of votes'. More important still, she stressed that 'you will never have human rights unless you have property rights'. On our policy towards the Soviets, she reinforced more or less what Hugh Seton-Watson and I had been saying (mentioning both of us and praising the work of our study group). 'Again, we have come to the same conclusion at the same time,' she said. Negotiate but be strong; do not try to achieve success by unilateral concessions. There was by now no evidence in her speech of any 'new approach' to the Kremlin. She was given a rapturous ovation.

For me the most remarkable feature about the PM's performance was the enormous respect she now commands not only among her supporters, but also among cynics and opponents – not that we had too many of the latter at the Hyde Park Hotel yesterday. There was a touch of sublimity to this gathering. As MT entered the hall everyone got up and stood for 20–30 seconds. That silent tribute was, in my reading, more than good manners or a gesture of obligatory support. It was homage paid to a woman who knows exactly what is ailing Britain and who is analytically rigorous and morally determined enough to impose her remedies. Such characteristics are rare in half-hearted and under-achieving Britain, but when they suddenly appear, and appear spectacularly concentrated in a woman, they attract admiration. I hesitate to liken her leadership to the rule of some 'Tyrannus' after periods of dissension in antiquity, but there was a whiff of a call for a Pisistratus in the air yesterday to ensure a spell of civilized but uncompromisingly firm order. I'm sure it will not last, for the British in their present decline are too feeble and frivolous to stomach the medicine for more than a short period, but it ought to do some good while it lasts.

Over drinks, having briefly exchanged pleasantries with the PM, I had a chat with Dennis Thatcher.

'I must congratulate you on your co-authorship of an apocryphal addition to *Yes, Prime Minister*.[1] Some of the papers claim that you wrote it jointly with the prime minister. I found it splendid and splendidly acted by her.'

'Not at all,' he said: 'it was entirely her doing. She wrote it all by herself.'

'The papers must have got it wrong.'

'The papers get all sorts of things wrong.'

'Whoever wrote it – it was a marvellous skit.'

---

1. Long-running, popular BBC television satire. Margaret Thatcher appeared with the two leading actors in a specially commissioned sketch.

'Oh, absolutely,' Dennis confirmed, 'and she acted it superbly. Do you know: they had only a single run-through. She memorized the words in one go and spoke them like an accomplished actress.'

'So it isn't true that she is a lady without that sense of self-mockery which people in this country count among the cardinal virtues?'

'Not at all. She is, you know, a wonderful woman. Whatever she sets her mind on, she will do and do brilliantly. She will tolerate no weaknesses in herself.'

'Trouble is,' he went on, 'she was born restless. She hates having time on her hands. She can't stay in one place for more than a day or two. An activist – with a vengeance,' he added, looking rather sorry for himself.

CHAPTER 4

A Call at Downing Street

With hindsight, I ought to have been aware earlier than I was that Margaret Thatcher's long and bitter struggle for a budgetary rebate from the European Community was not about British overpayment at all. Rather was it her way of expressing her growing hostility to a supranational institution which Britain had failed to join at its inception and was unable to influence the way she would have liked. Foreigners had made the rules – Britain had to live by them. Could there be a greater indignity?

In 1983–84, however, Margaret Thatcher's visceral dislike of a unifying Western Europe did not – yet – translate into Western Europe's dislike of a visceral Margaret Thatcher, even though her rough negotiating style was alienating almost every European head of government. In the eyes of the average Italian, German or Frenchman, the British prime minister was a *phénomène* – an intriguing mixture of clarity of mind, insolence, resolve and feminine guile the like of which could not be found in any other European capital. She and her 'ism' were a challenging thing, a very European thing, which the stick-in-the-mud British were thought no longer capable of producing. Continental Europe relished the spectacle.

Nor was her forthright language about the Soviet Union matched by anyone in high places on the Continent. Western Europe may have been terrified of the prospect of a military conflict with Moscow, but it loved the words of condemnation of the communist dictatorship freely flowing from the lips of this well-coiffured and gutsy lady. For one reason or another, Margaret Thatcher was riding high in the West European imagination. A weak Britain had suddenly acquired an unquantifiable asset – on a mere 42 per cent of the popular vote. But how was this to be turned to good account?

I felt the moment was right to attempt to wean Margaret Thatcher away from her offshore nationalism, presenting her with a view of Europe, and of her potential role in Europe, which would be worthy of her high opinion of herself. A doomed attempt, to be sure, by one man of little influence, but I went ahead regardless.

Diary

19 October 1984

Drove to No. 10 mid-morning. Found the whole of Downing Street heavily guarded by police. A new iron gate and railings have been erected; everyone was being checked. The IRA's Brighton bomb attack is only a week (12 October) behind us – the security people appear to have learned some lessons. Or have they?

As I was getting out of my taxi and a policeman was radioing through to No. 10 to clear me for entry, another cab drew up close to mine with a smarty-boots driver at the wheel but no passenger. Inside the passenger compartment: four hefty paper-sacks of the sort used for the transportation of coal or potatoes. A music-hall kind of a dialogue followed.

'Where're you going, mate?'

'No. 10, guv.'

'And what've you got inside those sacks?'

'Potatoes'.

'Potatoes?'

'Yes, someone in No. 10 must have ordered spuds for the missus to make the dinner with ...'

'OK, hang on a sec – I'll check it out.'

I was a little puzzled. Could it be that four big sacks of an unexamined load would be dumped in the prime minister's official residence so soon after a near fatal terrorist attempt on her life?

'Jim,' I heard the officer saying, 'I've got a cabbie here with some potatoes. Anyone ordered four sacks of spuds?'

'They don't know anything about it,' he turned to the driver. 'You're sure the load is for No. 10?'

'Sure, mate, see, it's been paid for. No one else's got the cash to pay in advance these days …'

'OK then, drive up to No. 10 over there and ring the bell.'

As I was slowly walking the forty-odd steps to No. 10, the taxi overtook me and arrived when I did. I was identified (by name only, no photograph, no passport, no ID card were required) and let in. But while a commissionaire was helping me with my coat and the door was left half ajar, I noticed that the cabbie began unloading, leaving the first sack just inside the reception hall. Another uniformed chap went to a telephone and rang presumably the kitchen or one of his superiors.

'I say, there is a taxi outside. Anyone ordered four sacks of potatoes?'

Back, apparently, came the answer that no one had. By that time the cabbie was heaving in a second sack and the matter of the order was once again subjected to discussion – without any result that I could make out, because, as I was being shown upstairs, the puzzled look continued on the faces of my dramatis personae, with by now two big sacks – of potatoes it was to be hoped – stood against the wall safely inside No. 10 Downing Street. I'm still unaware of how the potatoes crisis ended. For all I know, the spuds may have been for the chancellor of the exchequer in No. 11 …

I found the whole thing both entertaining and infuriating. Entertaining, because it would be grist to the mill of the 'quaint old England' school of American tourist who sees us as an operetta kingdom off the shores of Europe. Infuriating, because it seemed to show a continuing unawareness of the determination of the IRA and a lack of rigour in enforcing existing security rules. And this seven days after the Brighton bomb! How easy it would have been to blow up No. 10. And how amateurish the whole procedure of ringing bells, opening doors and delivering potatoes through the main entrance to the nerve-centre of the British government. Even my own identification was too flimsy for my taste. How could the police be sure that I really was who I said I was? I'm not a public figure and no documents were asked for. It was taken for granted that the

77

appointment I had made over the telephone had in fact been made by me. Had anyone chosen to impersonate me, he could have made it to the PM's presence without difficulty. Neither the IRA nor the Philby–Maclean–Blunt blunders seem to have taught us very much.

I was shown to the first-floor library cum waiting-room. On a shelf prominently displayed: a piece of blackish moon-rock under a glass bubble, donated to Margaret Thatcher by Nixon. After a short wait I was escorted up two further flights of stairs and then to the PM's study. Margaret Thatcher, seated at a large writing desk at the far end of the room, got up motioning me to the coffee table. 'Hello, George, how are you, come and sit down, tell me what you have been doing.'

She did not look at all well, but after her Brighton ordeal, nothing could be less surprising. Her eyes were giving her trouble. The horrors of the last several days were etched on her face. She had lost several friends; others were terribly injured and she herself had had a very narrow escape. But within minutes of the explosion, in the early hours of last Friday, she gave interviews, and only a few hours later she addressed the Conservative Party Conference as though nothing unusual had happened. Her nerve and self-control were most admirable.

I said I was grateful for the time she was giving me. Even half an hour in the wake of such an outrage was a generous allocation. I'd come to speak about Europe, I said, and the enormous respect she commanded in all parts of the Continent. Living in Munich and travelling widely, I was convinced that now would be the time to take a fresh look at our attitude to the EEC. I then gave her a somewhat overdrawn picture of how she figured in most 'ordinary' Europeans' imagination – as the only 'man' in any European cabinet when it came to confronting the USSR; as a stateswoman rather than a passing figure in the whirlpool of politics; as the author of a concise and radical 'conservative' political agenda, and as Europe's potentially most effective link with the Americans because of the British–American connection.

Haggling with Brussels, I said, about the price of butter, about CAP,[1] about budget rebates and the like should not exhaust the British government's powers to shape European policies. So utilitarian a purpose limits British horizons and creates bad blood on the Continent at a time when Britain could benefit from the priceless popularity she, as prime minister, enjoys everywhere, even, as I told her quoting an example, in Switzerland.

But I went further: please imagine, I said, the historic role you and under your premiership this country could play if you assumed the leadership of European unification. What a fine part for a person of your vision, your enthusiasm and your political touch. What a constructive contribution to relaunching the faltering ship of NATO. What is required is a re-think of our policies *vis-à-vis* the EEC. We have to create a psychological climate in which British interests are seen by public opinion to be inalienable parts of European interests, and vice versa. And that, in my opinion, is what they are. I even suggested that she should undertake a Euro-tour and make a number of Euro-speeches which would pick up all the principal themes on the European agenda: the case for a joint foreign and defence policy; the oneness of our culture; the need to think of Eastern Europe as lands only temporarily cut off from what used to be Christendom; the need to stop the plundering of our planet, and so on.

For Eastern and Central Europeans, I said, the idea of a united Europe has enormous magnetism. They want desperately to get out of Soviet occupation and tutelage and belong to that magical thing: Europe, a club of the élite to which they think they rightfully belong. And so they do. We should bear in mind that Czechs, Poles and Hungarians have always been organic parts of Europe, and sooner or later they will have to be reintegrated.

Having just paid an official visit to Hungary, the PM would, so I was hoping, understand all this well enough. I had supplied a number of themes for her Hungarian speeches, some of which made similar points.

---

1. Common Agricultural Policy.

I didn't, alas, put my 'message' very coherently. I felt the half-hour deadline was pressing against me, and that others with weightier business were waiting to see the PM. In any case, who was I to tender uninvited advice on a matter so momentous? As a man of Hungarian birth, I've always exercised restraint in offering advice to my native British friends about all things relating to British sovereignty. I carry a British passport and a set of deeply European convictions, but sovereignty is something for the family council, to which outsiders, even naturalized outsiders, do not belong. I wish I'd been able to live up to this fine distinction more convincingly than I have.

The PM listened to my oration rather passively. I could sense that she appreciated what I was saying about the respect she commands on the Continent, especially Germany. But she seemed cool to my policy suggestions. I said: 'Prime Minister, no one in Europe has the political charisma you have. You could be a trustee of European culture, a custodian of European history and tradition, and a bridge between Europe and the US – if only you decided to grasp the opportunity and identify yourself with the European problematik.'

'Well, George, all this sounds very attractive, and I appreciate what you are saying; but I'm a little wary of taking on this European past. What would it mean? Making speeches, wouldn't it?'

'Well, making speeches would obviously be involved, but it would not be just that.'

'Ah, I've just been invited to make a speech in Bonn but declined. I have made so many of these European speeches that I couldn't face another. So I asked Geoffrey Howe to go to Bonn and do it for me. What's the point of uttering another string of platitudes?'

'But wouldn't you say that making speeches of the right sort built on a new policy could be extremely important?' I said. 'They would make Europeans feel that someone commanding great authority, someone they respect and admire, does understand their concerns about war and peace, the nuclear factor in the civilian economy, the degradation of the environment etc. And wouldn't that be a constructive as well as a pleasant thing to do?'

I didn't say that it would also secure for Margaret Thatcher a very special niche in history, but that was clearly my meaning. I was hoping that my appeal to her vanity would prove stronger than her backward-looking view of Europe. I may have overdone my *captatio benevolentiae*, but I felt the stakes were high. I would have loved to see her as 'Queen' of Europe, rather than a carping voice from an island coven. It was that desire that prompted me to come to London.

'How do you see the situation in Germany?' she asked.

'It may not be obvious to the untrained eye, but, behind the backs of the Soviets, German unification is in fact quietly happening apace through a fast-growing number of economic ties, personal contacts and, of course, through the exceptional status GDR exports enjoy on the markets of the EEC. We can already talk of a latent form of German unification.'

'What's so latent about it?' the PM asked. 'We have known all about it for a long time, and we'd better be on our guard.'

This, and Margaret Thatcher's tone, surprised me. I had expected that drawing the GDR into the Western orbit by stealth, as it were, would meet with her approval. It was, after all, going to be a blow to the cohesion of the Soviet empire and a great plus for the Alliance. Not so.

To balance her suspicions, I then told the PM that the German people were especially impressed by her record. They liked a clear-headed leader. They admired the way in which she dealt with the unions, her resolve to restore British sovereignty in the Falklands, her philosophy of self-reliance, and, in the last week, her unflapp-ability after the Brighton bombing.

'What I find a little upsetting', I said, 'is the German Left's attitude to America. There is anti-Americanism among the chatter-ing classes just as there is in France, too, but in Germany it is aggravated by the fear of the installation of medium-range nuclear weapons and the prospect of annihilation-without-consultation. The spread of American junk culture is another source of anti-American feeling, but this, too, is as common in France as it is in Germany.'

'Well, I can't understand that,' she said. 'The Germans have been built up by the Americans, protected by the Americans and are still relying on the Americans for their security. Weinberger[1] was here the other day and this is what he told me: "If you people in Europe don't want our protection, we'll just pack it in and go. We don't like to be uninvited guests and protect people against their will." You know, George, the Germans should take note of that. They do have to bear in mind that the Americans might just pack their bags one fine day and go. They cannot just become an outsize Switzerland, an unguided missile.'

I could sense animus. I mentioned the centrality of Germany to all our concerns and the great financial contribution the Germans have been making to European unification. This did not go down well either.

'It's always been a misnomer to say that the Germans are the paymasters of Europe. The Germans have been simply paying reparations for all the things they did during the war; we couldn't call it that, but that is what they have been doing.'

'Isn't it true', she asked, 'that the German Greens are in the forefront of feeding anti-American sentiment?'

'Yes, there is some truth in that,' I said, 'but the Greens are not a significant force. They are certainly *a* force one has to reckon with and they may grow stronger. But the people supporting them could be weaned away if the right policies were put in train and the right words were spoken. Their appeal rests on their criticism of polluting industries, of unlimited growth, of the devastation of the forests and so on. Personally,' I said blowing my own horn, 'I understand their worries. In 1971 I published a symposium in which these concerns were addressed. I called it *Can We Survive our Future?*[2] long before Greens as an organized force were known in Europe. The German Greens' anti-Americanism is a by-product of their ecological fears – Americans, in their view, being the world's most reckless polluters.'

---

1. Caspar Weinberger, US secretary of defence, 1981–87.
2. With Michael Glenny.

'Well,' the PM observed, 'the pollution can be controlled and the acid rain eliminated if we stop car emissions and rule out coal and oil as our main sources of energy. But that means using nuclear power, and the Greens want that even less! So, if we were to follow the Green ideology, there could be no solution to our problems. We would have to de-industrialize and stop moving about as individuals.'

'That is true,' I answered, 'but, with respect, it is nevertheless important that we should publicly recognize the Greens' concerns, for they are shared by many millions of people in Germany and the rest of Europe. The Germans are idealistic people. Their idealism can take different forms. Their environmental anxiety is one benign manifestation of it, their identification with the European idea is another. We should sympathize with both lest disillusion at the impotence of democracy and of Europe should reawaken sentiments of an intolerant nationalistic kind. Happily, they are now conspicuously absent.'

'You know I never believed that German nationalism was dead,' Margaret Thatcher said. 'Nor did I believe that it would be dormant for a long time. I always thought that when the next German generation were old enough to think and lead the country, the drive to reunite Germany would be there again. But we don't want that because there is no question that if the Germans were reunited they would, once again, dominate the whole of Europe.

'Don't be misled by phrases and purple prose,' she went on; 'the Europeans don't feel that European solidarity is a real thing. They don't think it is tangible. Schmidt and Mitterrand[1] will speak about it at the drop of a hat. They are very good at rhetoric and crafting phrases that sound appealing to the French and the Germans but have no resonance in English ears. Have you ever seen them negotiating about European questions of allegedly joint concern? *I* have – most recently at an economic summit conference. You ought to have seen how bitterly they contested every single issue. That didn't convince me that their hearts are in the supra-national idea. They

---

1. François Mitterrand, French president, 1974–89.

83

are simply out to get the best deal they can for their own country, as governments always have done.'

'Talking about European anti-Americanism,' I said, 'one could claim, if one were to make hazardous generalizations, that Europeans are cultural pessimists while the Americans are cultural optimists. This makes Americans look shallow if not foolish in European eyes, and not just in Germany. The French take the same view, and if polls are to be trusted the British are no different. It explains, though it does not excuse, the Europeans' America-baiting. There is', I said, 'also some truth in the old dictum "help a man and he'll never forgive you". Perhaps the Americans have helped us too often.'

The PM, understandably, seemed disinclined to be lured by my bait and enter a philosophical discussion. She said, 'It is quite natural that the Americans should be cultural optimists. They have enormous and mostly sparsely populated territories on their borders. To the North they have a friendly nation, Canada, which has never given them trouble and to the South they have Mexico and the smaller states of Central America which have, until quite recently, given them few sleepless nights. *Of course* they are optimists. They don't know what fear of invasion *is*; whereas in Europe we have always been living cheek by jowl, country to country, and suffered invasion after invasion, aggression after aggression. No wonder we are pessimists.'

Time was pressing. I had it on the tip of my tongue that cultural optimism and pessimism were not simply functions of geography or even of war and peace – although all three were extremely important – and that I didn't think cultural pessimism was necessarily a bad thing. Indeed, it often coincides with the most fertile cultural periods. But all of this would have taken us into another topic.

The PM came back to the state of the USSR. What did I make of it? I said Murray Feschbach's[1] recent studies of health care and social conditions in the Soviet Union painted a devastating picture;

---

1. American scholar, writer on Soviet health and social problems.

diseases we had thought extinct (TB, diphtheria, etc.) were re-surfacing; life expectancy was coming down (especially for men); hospitals were in a pitiable state; medicines were in short supply; social care was atrocious; infant mortality was higher even than in any of the satellites, and so on. We had Feschbach in Munich recently, I said, and I heard him personally confirm his various findings.

What did it all mean? the PM wanted to know.

I don't think we should conclude, I said, that the Soviet system is on the verge of collapse because of these social ills and medical shortcomings. There is in America, especially in certain departments of the CIA, a school of thinking which holds that it is. But this is looking at Soviet conditions through American spectacles – a notoriously flawed premiss. The Russian people have a well-attested capacity for putting up with hardship. They did so during the Civil War, in the Second World War and during agricultural collectiviza-tion in the early 1930s. A shortage of needles and antibiotics will not make them rise against the system. If and when communism does collapse, it will be for wider reasons such as the exhaustion of the system's legitimacy, self-doubt among the leaders and a non-performing economy. It is on these issues that we should press them.

The PM asked whether I could send her copy of Feschbach's writings. I'll do so as soon as I'm back in Munich.

Had I seen Jeane Kirkpatrick lately? 'Yes,' I said, 'only a couple of days ago in Paris. She was being awarded the Hachette Prize in the presence of a high-powered political and intellectual audience.'

'What are her chances of being appointed to a post in government other than her present embassy at the UN?'

I said I could not tell, but she was clearly very close to Reagan.

'At the presentation ceremony in Paris,' I said, 'the principal eulogy was Reagan's. He had sent along a video-recorded message displayed on a vast screen giving Jeane extraordinary praise. He described her as a wonderful ambassador, a leading political thinker, a great initiator of policies – one of the great Americans. "She belongs to that great generation of women whom all admire and who have made history: Prime Minister Margaret Thatcher, Mrs Golda Meir[1] and now Ambassador Jeane Kirkpatrick".'

The PM looked at me with a twinkle in her eye: 'Well, Indira Gandhi[2] isn't going to like that, is she?' Here was the feminine side of Margaret Thatcher.

She then asked how I saw the situation in Eastern Europe. I said three recent visits – Kádár's[3] to Mitterrand (16 October), Ceauşescu's to Kohl[4] (15–17 October) and Honecker's to Finland (17–18 October) – were indications that despite the expiry of *détente*, despite the cool climate between Washington and Moscow and the virtual revival of the Cold War, there was some leeway for independent East European statesmanship. Certainly Kádár and Ceauşescu were trying to distance themselves from the Kremlin, and we ought to encourage and reward that.

The PM nodded in agreement. 'We must exploit their differences', she said, 'without egging them on to rebellion. We do differentiate in our policies. Liberalization in human rights, any promotion of pluralism do earn rewards from us and will continue to do so.' I said this was, in fact, also our broadcasting policy in Munich.

My time was nearly up. She escorted me to the door. 'It was very nice seeing you again, George. And if you have any papers you want me to read – a summary of your suggestions or anything else for that matter – please send them along. I have fond memories of our cooperation at the time of the Churchill speech.

'And please remember: I feel very strongly that the Atlantic Alliance is most important, even though I also feel that the Americans have done us a disservice by invading Grenada. But – I have learnt to think that this is how very large powers behave. Morality does not really come into the picture. The more the pity.'

1. Prime minister of Israel, 1969–74.

2. Indian prime minister, 1966–77, 1980–84.

3. János Kádár, first secretary of the Central Committee, Hungarian Socialist Workers' Party, 1956–85, general secretary, 1985–88.

4. Helmut Kohl, chancellor of the German Federal Republic, 1982– .

I left with a sense of some dissatisfaction. I hadn't marshalled my arguments well and felt I was a bit of an intruder at a busy time. Downstairs, on my way out, I found a large delegation waiting to see her. This was also the day of the Anglo-Italian summit.

Why the prime minister did not put me off until a less busy time in her diary, I can only guess at. Perhaps she wanted to show herself totally uncowed after Brighton, in which she succeeded brilliantly. Perhaps, after the horrors of recent days, she needed supportive company, which I hope I provided.

I was nevertheless slightly annoyed that there was no opportunity for a more comprehensive discussion. The strength of the PM's views about Europe and Germany came as a surprise. I found them disturbing. I will now send her a summary of the ideas I put to her so imperfectly and fill in Charlie Douglas-Home. He may, with luck, recycle some of my suggestions in *The Times* to much better effect, as he has done on previous occasions.

26 October 1984

This morning I sent the prime minister, through Hugh Thomas, a summary of the points I was trying to make at No. 10. I'll be sending a copy to Charlie. He and Jessica[1] have become close friends. Charlie shares my strong views about the Soviet Union. It remains to be seen how close we are on the future of Europe. Charlie is extremely ill. He is permanently in a wheelchair and spends the odd day in hospital for I believe chemotherapy. Having him as an ally – and what a courteous and strong-minded ally he is – is a delight. He is having an endless quarrel with Richard Davy[2] about our Soviet policy. I hope and pray Charlie will last.

This is what I said in my memorandum, accompanied by a short covering letter, to the prime minister:

---

1. Jessica Douglas-Home, writer on communist affairs, head of the Eminescu human rights group, widow of Charles Douglas-Home.
2. Senior journalist and leader-writer of *The Times*.

6 October 1984

1. Trust in the legitimacy of the Alliance is being eroded on both sides of the Atlantic.

2. The present American political class is poor at explaining the rationale of US policies and the character of American society to its West European partners. The Europeans, on their part, doubt the maturity, responsibility and predictability of the American political establishment.

   The result is mutual suspicion: complacency about the Soviet threat in Western Europe, and scepticism about the loyalty and staying power of the West Europeans in the US.

3. But mutual incomprehension goes beyond the political and military domain. Much of it is psychological and cultural. The Americans feel that an ungrateful and short-sighted Western Europe wants to enjoy the fruits of security without sharing the costs and risks that make security possible, especially outside the NATO area. The West Europeans fear that their continent has been reduced to the status of a mere 'theatre' in American thinking, to be fought over and, if necessary, destroyed as America's first line of defence.

4. The US–European relationship is anomalous for yet another reason. The US is the first world-power in modern history that is reluctant to be a world-power and has no ideological blueprint for the rest of mankind. Western Europe is the first great economic power in history unable or unwilling to translate its economic muscle into political identity and military power. The Europeans cannot understand why the Americans are reluctant to 'lead'. The Americans do not comprehend why the Europeans cannot be equal partners and respond, as their interests demand, to the Soviet challenge on a worldwide scale.

5. Behind these obvious and less obvious factors there is also a good deal of plain prejudice. Prejudice, however, is a powerful force in human affairs. It shapes history; we ignore it at our peril.

   There is a feeling in Western Europe that America's brash optimism cannot do justice to the problems of old and sophisticated societies; that the Americans' forthright 'problem-solving' approach does not apply to the intricacies of European life and culture.

   In American eyes, on the other hand, much of Europe is an outdoor museum – to be admired, to be sure, but not to be taken entirely seriously. They see the European way of life as 'élitist' and the Euro-

88

peans' attitude to industry and enterprise as antiquated and even comical.

6. Britain is a bridge between these two worlds. Rightly or wrongly, she enjoys a reputation for political experience and wisdom. To that has now been added a new factor: the standing and indeed the charisma of the British Prime Minister. Alone among European politicians, Margaret Thatcher carries authority and commands respect both in Western Europe and the US. She is widely admired even by those who do not share her politics. She is seen as a leader cast in the mould of Churchill. She could command loyalty beyond the shores of the United Kingdom. These are powerful factors that the Western world could turn to good account.

7. What is needed is a British initiative, led by the Prime Minister, to give Europe an identity both more tangible and more readily exploitable than that possessed by the EEC.

One way of doing that would be a 'tour of Europe', or several 'tours of Europe', by the Prime Minister. She would speak to the people of each West European country and address herself to a number of themes that cut across borders. These might include the fear of nuclear war, the state of the environment, the depersonalization of life in technological society, the impact of the electronic media on democratic societies and others. She would, and she alone could, capture the imagination of those millions for whom the appeal of Europe has long been buried under butter-mountains or drowned in wine-lakes.

8. By identifying Britain with these common concerns of Europeans, the Prime Minister would stand to acquire the necessary legitimacy to represent the 'responsible face' of Europe in the eyes of Americans, and to interpret US interests to America's European partners in a manner that the latter could accept. She, unlike some of her predecessors, would then not be looked upon as a Trojan horse by the European public.

9. Mrs Thatcher has a unique opportunity to do what Churchill missed doing: to put a British Prime Minister at the head of a great continent in the common interests of Europe, the US and, indeed, Western civilization.

CHAPTER 5

From an Austrian Resort

Margaret Thatcher's requests for advice or speech-writing assistance were striking by their informality. A broadly shared political platform and the right personal chemistry were enough to induce her to entrust her unceasing search for fresh thought to a small number of private sympathizers. The more detached these were from Whitehall, and the more unversed in the ways of the Conservative Party, the more she seemed to value their judgement. So much informality left me, for one, at times a little exasperated.

Diary

Munich, 26 February 1985

This will have to be a condensed entry about my (small) part in the prime minister's speech to the two houses of the US Congress on 20 February 1985.

Pat and I were preparing for a week's skiing in Wagrain in Austria when, shortly before our departure, Charles Powell[1] came on the line asking on behalf of the PM whether I would assist her with her forthcoming American address. I said I'd be very happy to even though it would have to be done from my vacation in Austria.

The snow reports were discouraging, so I felt I'd have time on my hands to come up with ideas. Also, after months of punishing work at the Radio, time to be spent on the moral high ground struck

---

1. Later Sir Charles Powell, foreign policy adviser to the prime minister, 1984–91.

me as eminently desirable. In any case: for good or for ill, I'm an enthusiast by nature; how could I not pick up the PM's invitation whatever the snow conditions?

She was and is my principal hope in our contest with the Soviet system; I would have done almost anything to promote what I believed were her policies towards the Kremlin.

'Can you give me some idea what, in broad outline, the PM is planning to talk about?' But Charles couldn't. He said she had one draft from the Foreign Office which she didn't much like. It was too matter-of-fact and too pedestrian. She thought I might supply some inspiration and 'poetry'. This was a remark I wasn't a bit unhappy to hear, but some indication at least of where she wanted to go would have been helpful. Would she wish to concentrate on East–West relations, the Anglo-American nexus, Europe? But Charles couldn't be drawn because I believe he genuinely didn't know. Charming and bright as always, he said rather disarmingly: 'Would you like to send us anything that you think would be relevant to the occasion and would lift the speech above our immediate concerns? We need a large, statesman-like view.'

This was an exceptionally vague 'brief' but none the worse for that. I knew by now that the PM would read and reflect and select and that was all right with me. To be part of the process of her articulations in causes I believed in was reward enough.

Charles said he would tell the PM that I would try to do as she asked, adding that in a week or two she might call a meeting to bring the various threads together. Two further prospective co-authors, Lord Hailsham and Lord Thomas, would also be present.

Wagrain was indeed having a poor season. What snow we had was slushy. It froze into icy moguls at night and turned into pools of water during the day. The rain didn't help. Pat and I nevertheless skied on relentless. Poor conditions have yet to frighten me off this most delightful of all sports. Early in the morning and at night I proceeded to write up three packages of ideas which I at least felt strongly about and were 'cold-warish' to a tee. They were meant to be additions to rather than replacements for the Foreign Office draft, for in the course of yet another telephone conversation Charles Powell finally told me that the mandarins had provided four 'challenges' on broadly geographical lines, but he didn't say what they were. The vagueness of it all was very British and maddening.

So on Monday 28 January I sent him, express, one broad theme which I had used before but which cannot, in my judgement, be used often enough *vis-à-vis* the Soviet system: how liberal democracy is *the* astonishing thing in modern life, and dictatorship the oldest of old hats. I had deployed this for MT in 1983, but re-articulating it to the morally sensitive American Congress could do no harm. I got it down on three pages just in time to catch the last collection in the village post office. I galloped down with it in the slush. After a day's skiing, and speech-writing at dawn and dusk, this final sprint to the nearest place to No. 10 Downing Street made me feel I was on top of the world. Perhaps I was a little *over* the top of the world, for my 'theme' contained some high-falutin rhetoric :-

> Let it be said about us by our successors that our nations were tolerant enough to be free; free enough to be strong; and strong enough to lead the world not by their strength but their example.
>
> That has always been America's special message to the world. Let it be the message of the whole free world. Let it be especially addressed to those who believe that some inevitable law in history works for our destruction and that it is their duty to play midwife to it. There is no such law in history and there is no call for such midwives.

Wisely, as I now think, the lady did not use these bits of my vapourings, although what I had written was relevant enough.

My second theme, sent off a couple of days later, was an attack on the left-liberal (mainly American) notion that there was 'moral equivalence' between the USSR and America; and the third stressed that while we find the philosophy of Marxism-Leninism false and its practice abhorrent, it is traditional Russian expansionism, using the passport of communism as its legitimation, that worries us most. Treaties and moral pledges, I wrote, are unlikely to change the character of the Soviet system; they have never done so before. We should nevertheless talk to the Kremlin while keeping our powder dry.

The whole draft ran to ten typed pages. Without the slightest notion of what MT had in mind, I was truly groping in the dark. Nor did I have a single book or any other reference materials to help me. I wrote down what *I* would have said to Congress in terms of my underlying philosophy, hoping it would not be too distant from the PM's. I was fully aware that she had no taste for ideological arguments, so I didn't give her any. At the same time, however, I was hoping she might build on the spirit of my reasoning. So it eventually turned out to be.

A few days after my return to Munich, my colleagues and I lunched with Alun Chalfont[1] and Frank Roberts[2], who were in town for our West European Advisory Council meeting. Chalfont told me that he, too, had been invited to contribute ideas for the PM's speech. There was going to be a preparatory session at Chequers, with himself and Hugh Thomas (Lord Hailsham wasn't mentioned) taking part. The circle was widening. I was being left out. This was disappointing but not unexpected – one of the penalties of not being in London. Or did I make a hash of my draft?

In the event, MT made an outstanding speech[3] in the presence of Vice-President Bush, but it was only vaguely related to what I had written. I was pleased and surprised by her enthusiastic support of European unification. After my session with her at No. 10 last October, I didn't expect her to make so forceful a case. She spoke about 'a visionary chapter' in our history. Her praise of integration didn't, alas, come from my pen; quite possibly Hugh Thomas was responsible, but Hugh and I are very close on Europe. It was her adoption of our argument that mattered:

For the first forty years of this century, there were seven great

---

1. Lord Chalfont, minister of state in the Foreign Office, 1964–70.
2. Sir Frank Roberts, former British ambassador to Yugoslavia, the Soviet Union and the Federal Republic of Germany.
3. Margaret Thatcher, *In Defence of Freedom: Speeches on Britain's Relations with the World 1976–1986*, London, 1986, pp. 106–15.

powers: the United States, Great Britain, Germany, France, Russia, Japan, Italy. Of those seven two now tower over the rest – the United States and the Soviet Union.

To that swift and historic change Europe – a Europe of many different histories and many different nations – has had to find a response. It has not been an easy passage to blend this conflux of nationalism, patriotism and sovereignty, into a European Community, yet I think our children and grandchildren may see this period – these birth pangs of a new Europe – more clearly than we do now. They will see it as a visionary chapter in the creation of a Europe able to share the load alongside you. Do not doubt the firmness of our resolve in the march towards this goal, but do not underestimate what we already do.

After our study group's meeting at the CPS in London the other day, Hugh asked whether I had heard from the PM. She had, he said, just returned from America and would certainly write.

'I don't think she used much of my draft but she made an excellent speech.'

'Oh, don't worry about that; this was a different sort of an occasion from the Churchill speech. Your suggestions went to Powell and he probably fashioned a speech out of the drafts he had received, helping himself on his way to some outside intellectual property,' Hugh said with a chuckle.

I hope, in fact I am fairly certain, this was not quite the case. Charles Powell is his own man; he can do without borrowed feathers. He may have been under orders to integrate the ideas the PM had asked for into a workable whole.

10 March 1985

This morning, to my surprise, a letter arrived from the PM through the Bonn Embassy. It is dated 22 February so she must have written it immediately upon her return. Thanking me for 'the excellent material' I had provided, she said, 'given how generous you have been with your inspiration, [I] can continue to draw on your thoughts for future speeches.'

CHAPTER 6

On the Lawn of
No. 10

Having helped to encourage the idea in the mind of Margaret Thatcher that close rapport should be the overriding aim of her first encounter with President Reagan, I was a little taken aback a few years later to see just how close and undignified that rapport was becoming on the part of the prime minister. There were, of course, sound political reasons for showing ostentatious friendship to a powerful man who was beginning to return it with interest. The president liked and respected Margaret Thatcher, and in the eyes of the public she cut a scintillating, royal figure against the drabness and vacuity of American politics. All that enhanced her enthusiasm.

But Margaret Thatcher was going too far. The sound of her all-encompassing obeisance – despite Grenada, despite the gas pipeline affair and other irritations – jarred on many ears in Britain and the rest of Europe. Her patriotic rhetoric notwithstanding, she was reducing the United Kingdom to the status of a client-state of America. Ronald Reagan was now her hero – fulsome praise of him her stock-in-trade. The tongue that seldom hesitated to lash out at the leaders of Western Europe was quietly respectful in front of the mighty transatlantic uncle – whether it was Ronald Reagan or George Bush. 'Mrs Thatcher, who can be so tough when she talks to her European partners, is like a little girl of eight years old when she talks to the president of the United States. You have to cock your ear to hear her, she's really so touching,' President Mitterrand is said to have observed to Jacques Attali in 1989.[1]

In the real world, the Anglo-American 'special relationship' was becoming one-sided to the point of embarrassment. British sovereignty was contingent and increasingly circumscribed. Any 'threat' to it was

---

1. Jacques Attali, *Verbatim III*, Paris, 1995, p. 271.

95

coming not from Europe, but from the inexorable realities of the modern world.

Diary

30 June 1988

Yesterday the PM gave a farewell garden-party for John O'Sullivan,[1] one of her most trusted lieutenants, now leaving her think-tank at No. 10. I have known John for several years and respect him greatly. He is a helpful and irrepressible comrade-in-arms in our battle with the Soviets. Much of the 'political class' was present; so were assorted pundits from high journalism, as well as lowbrows of less reputable journalistic provenance together with their ladies in their finery.

Having done some of her rounds, the PM drew me aside. Then for some twenty minutes we stood almost motionless on the lawn, to the great discomfort of my sore hip. Friends and foes alike were giving us enquiring glances from a distance: whatever could they be talking about for so long? I must have risen in their ratings.

The PM was in search of sympathetic company and she knew I was a good listener. She dilated with enthusiasm on Reagan's visit to Britain – he has clearly become her hero – and the time he and Nancy Reagan had spent in the prime ministerial flat in No. 10.

'There we were sitting upstairs,' she said with reverence, pointing to what looked to me like a modest establishment in the attic; 'the president was in expansive mood. He was reminiscing and telling jokes. In the garden down here we had a Guards' band, and when President Reagan recognized a favourite tune, he would sing. It was a marvellous occasion! President Reagan is a warm person, very informal, witty to a degree and intellectually much underrated.'

This fawning praise was just a little too much for me. Why 'President' Reagan all the time? Our no-nonsense prime minister, so ready with her tongue in Parliament and *vis-à-vis* Europeans, has

---

1. Writer and journalist, member of the prime minister's Policy Unit.

been overawed by the charm and power of the American. But this was a garden-party – so I said nothing.

The PM was then wondering aloud what I thought about the BBC Russian Service. Her reason for asking was a BBC Russian phone-in programme she had been invited to host. Should she do it?

I said the BBC Russian Service was greatly respected in the USSR as a source of factual information and thoughtful comment. True, I used to have reservations about the morally uncommitted line taken by one of its commentators in years past, but that, I said, took away little from the excellence of the service as a whole. When *Doctor Zhivago* was published in the West – and proscribed in the Soviet Union – the BBC broadcast, through the jamming, most of the novel back to Russia in the Russian language. And that, I said, was only one of many effective things the BBC was doing to neutralize Soviet censorship and penetrate the Iron Curtain.

'So, you'd advise me to do it. You see, I've seen and heard so many things on the BBC that infuriate me almost every day of the week – tendentious reporting, unfair comment, unbearable violence and vulgarity – that I hesitate to say yes when any part of the BBC asks me to do *anything*.'

I assured the PM that the BBC External Services in Bush House were under a completely separate management from the rest of the corporation, and were imbued with a spirit hardly different from the one that animated Radio Free Europe. Bush House was in the forefront of the West's battle of ideas and carried enormous influence throughout the world. I could see nothing but good coming out of her participation in the phone-in programme. It would be important, however (I added), to be prepared for the kind of questions Soviet listeners, now that they felt freer to speak their minds, might fire at her, for I was certain they would grab the opportunity to address difficult ones to the British prime minister.

At this point we were interrupted by Norman Tebbit[1] pushing

---

1. Lord Tebbit of Chingford, former chairman of the Conservative Party and cabinet minister.

his wife in a wheelchair, followed somewhat hesitantly, at a distance, by George Weidenfeld.[1] Here comes relief, I thought, as my hip was by now hurting unbearably. Despite her wretched condition, Mrs Tebbit was holding up well. She had been most seriously injured in the Brighton bombing and may never be able to walk again.

MT spoke to her briefly but with great warmth, and then turned to Tebbit. 'Norman, how is your book coming along?'

'It's been going well, thank you; in fact, it's finished.'

'Have you a title for it?'

'Yes, we are calling it *Upwardly Mobile*.'

'And who is your publisher?'

'Oh, he is right here behind me,' pointing to George Weidenfeld who was walking up to us with his best 'always-ready-to-serve-you' smile on his face.

'Well,' she said, wagging a finger at both, 'no kiss-and-tell story, I hope! We've had enough of those. They may be money-spinners, but they're a disgrace, an absolute disgrace.'

'Of course not,' Weidenfeld protested sheepishly.

Here was a chance for me to slip away and give my aching hip a rest.

---

1. Lord Weidenfeld of Chelsea, publisher and historian.

CHAPTER 7

A Memorable Lunch
at No. 10

Though Margaret Thatcher's strident speech at the College of Europe in Bruges, in September 1988, was indication enough that her hostility to European integration was increasingly fed by emotion, it could still not be inferred without further evidence that, wrapped within that hostility, another and more insidious aversion was powerfully alive: her atavistic fear of Germany and her suspicion of the German people *qua* people. This was an ugly thing, known but to a few, and unmentionable in decent company. It was to end Nicholas Ridley's career.[1]

But when the Soviet empire began to crumble, in the autumn of 1989, that fear immediately broke surface. Solemn Western commitments to bring a single Germany about were to be ignored or watered down, and the search for a new balance-of-power politics was at once to be set in train, with Margaret Thatcher herself trying to drive it forward almost single-handed. Fortunately for the future peace of

---

1. In July 1990, Nicholas Ridley, secretary of state for trade and industry, and a close friend of the prime minister, was forced to resign from Margaret Thatcher's government because of certain comments he had made about Germany in the weekly journal the *Spectator* (14 July 1990). On Monetary Union: 'This is all a German racket designed to take over the whole of Europe. It has to be thwarted. ... The deutschmark is always going to be the strongest currency, *because of their habits.*' On European integration: 'I'm not against giving up sovereignty in principle, but not to this lot. You might just as well give it to Adolf Hitler, frankly.' On Europe's post-communist architecture: 'It has always been Britain's role to keep these various powers balanced, and never has it been more necessary than now, with Germany so uppity,' etc. Dominic Lawson, editor of the journal, commented: 'Mr Ridley's confidence in expressing his views on the German threat must owe a little something to the knowledge that they are not significantly different from those of the prime minister ... even though in public she is required not to be so indelicate as to draw comparisons between Herren Kohl and Hitler.'

Europe, the search proved futile, but that it should have been attempted at a time when the true British interest demanded making constructive use of the opportunities created by the collapse of the Soviet super-power, left some of Britain's allies and many of the prime minister's supporters exasperated. Had it not been for the weakness of British influence and the foresight and great skill of the American diplomatic establishment – not least of President Bush[1] – an opening of historic proportions would have been missed. President Mitterrand 'made the wrong decision for France', she observes in her memoirs; 'closer Franco-British defence cooperation' was to be immediately considered.[2] Margaret Thatcher was on the warpath.

What stood out was her feverish and at times devious resistance to a development she was powerless to stop, and her isolation in trying to do so. Underlying it all was her poor comprehension of and lack of sympathy with the spirit of the whole postwar architecture of Western Europe.

If her Bruges speech was a mistake and a prelude to her fall, her German policy was a blow to Britain's long-term interests. The revolutionary changes in the Soviet domains had caught the British government entirely unprepared. True, all Western governments were suffering from a similar affliction, but in its effort to thwart the reunification of Germany, Whitehall ended up standing alone.

George Bush; after serious misgivings, François Mitterrand and Giulio Andreotti;[3] and, of course, contrary to British and French expectations, Mikhail Gorbachev and Eduard Shevardnadze[4] – the latter at their historic meeting with Helmut Kohl, Hans-Dietrich Genscher[5] and Horst Teltschik[6] at Achiz in the Caucasus in July 1990[7] – all eventually agreed to the creation of a single German state and the inclusion of that state in NATO. The British objections were ignored, though, in Germany, the mentality in which they had been conceived would long be

---

1. See Philip Zelikow and Condoleezza Rice, *Germany Unified and Europe Transformed, A Study in Statecraft*, Cambridge, Mass., 1995.
2. *The Downing Street Years*, London, 1993, p. 798.
3. Italian prime minister, 1972–73; 1976–79; 1989–92.
4. Minister of foreign affairs, USSR, 1985–90, later president of Georgia.
5. Foreign minister of the German Federal Republic, 1974–92.
6. Under-secretary of state, German federal chancellor's office, 1982–90.
7. For an authentic, indeed breathtaking, account, see Horst Teltschik, *329 Tage*, Innenansichten der Einigung, Berlin, 1991, pp. 319–45.

remembered. As Margaret Thatcher herself acknowledged: 'If there is one instance in which a foreign policy I pursued met with unambiguous failure, it was my policy on German re-unification.'[1]

We can surely agree with that, but there was nothing pre-ordained about her 'unambiguous failure'. More imagination, less nostalgia for the past, and a more courageous cabinet would have served Britain better than the visceral reactions of its famous but misguided prime minister. Not for the first time in our century, the tyranny of history was playing havoc with the judgement of British politicians.

Diary

Tuesday 19 December 1989

The occasion [on the previous day, 18 December] was the prime minister's lunch for members of the board of directors of the Centre for Policy Studies: Lord Thomas (chairman), Sir Ronald Halstead (treasurer; deputy chairman, British Steel), Sir Charles Tidbury (chairman, Whitbreads), David Willetts (CPS director of studies),[2] Ken Minogue (London School of Economics), Oliver Knox (CPS director of publications), and myself. The PM was assisted by Sir Geoffrey Howe (deputy prime minister, formerly foreign secretary) as well as Brian Griffiths (head of the PM's Policy Unit),[3] Mark Lennox-Boyd, the PM's parliamentary and private secretary,[4] and John Whittingdale, the PM's political secretary.[5]

I happened to coincide on the staircase with Charles Tidbury. 'What is our lunch about?', I asked. 'Do we have a game-plan?' He laughed: 'Oh, we haven't. Don't you know? Our job is to *listen*.'

I had tried to get hold of Hugh Thomas (never an easy matter) to see whether we should put our heads together and discuss what on earth we were going to talk about. In the event we had two short

---

1. *The Downing Street Years*, p. 813.
2. Later Conservative MP.
3. Later Lord Griffiths of Fforestfach.
4. Later Sir Mark Lennox-Boyd.
5. Later Conservative MP.

chats on the phone. 'Well, it's not really necessary,' Hugh said, 'she will tell us what's on her mind and then we'll just deploy our arguments and talk.' It had, in fact, been like that on one or two previous occasions, and that's how it turned out to be on this one. But I was a little uncomfortable with the idea of our rather in-cohesive board facing the PM, her deputy and some of the best brains in her service without preparation.

We were having drinks when the PM joined us accompanied by Geoffrey Howe; she made a bee-line for the little group I was in; she came straight to me, greeting everyone on the way, and said with considerable excitement: 'George, here we are; we've now got trouble in Romania, too – have you heard that there are demonstrations in Timişoara and Arad? Troops have apparently surrounded the two cities and there is some priest or other in Timişoara whom the local Hungarians are trying to defend against deportation.'[1] 'Yes, I've heard about it,' I said. In fact, unrest in Timişoara had started a couple of nights earlier, but the news services were slow to pick it up. So we began talking about Eastern Europe. The PM was ex-uberant about the prospect of the destabilisation of the Ceauşescu regime. She made some pointed observations about Ceauşescu's tyranny: this was the last bastion of old-fashioned Stalinism, it had to come down, the Soviets would not prop it up, and so on. I wholly agreed, adding only half in jest, 'Wouldn't it be a nice irony if Soviet tanks appeared in the streets of Bucharest to be greeted as liberators?!'

She then launched into German reunification. Here I found an unexpected ally in David Willetts. What did we think about it? the PM asked. David said he thought unification would be a good thing; true, it had to be done circumspectly, but it was, in any case, unstoppable; at which the PM threw up her hands in horror: 'No, not at all.' It was clear – it became even clearer during lunch – that she was hostile to the whole idea on the grounds of a rather old-fashioned nationalism. Indeed, the stridency one could detect in

---

1. Pastor, later Bishop, László Tőkés.

some of the PM's statements in the last year or so came out with full
force during our discussion. She felt she was among friends and
could let her hair down. I was amazed to hear her uttering views
about people and countries, especially Germany, which were not all
that different from the Alf Garnett[1] version of history.

'Well, George, what do *you* think?' she went on. I made a point
similar to David's: reunification was indeed unstoppable but also
desirable. We were, I said, committed to unification by a dozen or
more pledges and declarations, not least under Germany's 1949 Basic
Law (Constitution) which came into being under Allied patronage.[2]
'Oh, no, no, no,' the PM shot back, 'we are committed to the
Helsinki Agreement in which the permanence of borders is affirmed
by thirty-five states. True,' she said, 'provision is made for the
peaceful change of borders, but apart from that we are committed to
upholding the borders as they are.' 'Yes,' I said, 'but, with respect,
we are also committed to German unification under NATO, then
the four-power German Treaty of (26 May) 1952, then the 1967
Harmel Report[3] reinforced by numerous declarations and speeches
by all Western leaders. A single and free Germany has been the
Allies' consistently declared objective since 1945, and we always said
it was the *absence* of such a united Germany that caused world
tension and instability.'

The PM did not like this. 'But we've never said by what processes
unification would be achieved,' she said, 'or on what time scale.'
Geoffrey Howe put his oar in: 'Well, yes, the Helsinki Agreement is

1. Abusive, bigoted character in a British television comedy series.
2. 'The entire German people is called upon to accomplish, by free self-
determination, the unity and freedom of Germany.' Preamble, last paragraph.
3. '... no final and stable settlement in Europe is possible without a solution
of the German question which lies at the heart of present tensions in Europe.
Any such settlement must end the unnatural barriers between Eastern and Western Europe, which are most clearly and cruelly manifested in the division of
Germany ... . The Allies will examine and review suitable policies designed to
achieve a just and stable order in Europe, to overcome the division of Germany
and foster European security.'
Articles 8 and 12, *Future Tasks of the Alliance*, Report of the North Atlantic
Council, December, 1967.

important, but it allows for the peaceful change of borders,' he said almost inaudibly. We cycled round the whole ground again. I observed that the Helsinki Agreement was not a binding international treaty but a mere declaration. Geoffrey Howe agreed, but said it could not be changed unless all parties concurred. It was a chaotic discussion – the sort one gets at stand-up sessions with drinks in hand. I have a great distaste for them.

What came out of all this was that the PM is extremely reluctant to see Germany assume a role other than that of a divided country, still controlled by the post-war arrangements, and indeed under *de facto* four-power occupation. Surprisingly for me, she came back to the point again and again that we had, in the four-power Berlin Agreement, a perfectly valid international instrument. This could, in her interpretation, be used by the four victorious powers to retain certain rights, and these rights could be enforced in an emergency. I found this preposterous and a sure prescription for disaster in terms of European unification and solidarity. The PM expressed surprise: 'Well, I'm really shocked to hear that George and David should be holding such views.'

'You know, George,' she said coming quite close to me, 'there are things that people of your generation and mine ought never to forget. We've been through the war and we know perfectly well what the Germans are like, and what dictators can do, and how national character doesn't basically change ...' and so on. This was disturbing. If the British prime minister feels these things to be true, then we are heading for an unregenerate Europe, and most of our work over the last thirty or forty years, from Monnet to the present day, will have been wasted. I only hope my fears are unfounded. Otherwise we will find ourselves back in 1910, and I said so to her in guarded language. We were in for a lively lunch.

At table the German question was in the forefront of MT's mind again. Oliver Knox came out on the PM's side: 'Yes, indeed,' he said, 'the Germans have to be watched.' Mrs Thatcher's words on Germany went on being loaded with anger – assertions rather than arguments: 'once a German, always a German'; 'You can never trust them', and so on. It is, she said, now within the Germans' power to expand into an economically dominant empire, and what they could not attain through world wars they would try to achieve through economic imperialism. The whole of Eastern Europe is going to be their bailiwick; they are already taking over East Germany; all of which is going to create a menace for Britain.

Hugh Thomas and I tried to put in a corrective: 'My impression has been', Hugh said, 'that NATO and our defences have been created because we were threatened by the Soviet Union. Have we switched enemies? Do we suddenly have a threat facing us in the centre of Europe, from Germany, our ally?' MT said: 'Well, we have always fought for a balance of power in Europe and that has to be established again and again; don't be deceived by words. As soon as the Germans have fully recovered they will reassert their hegemonic interests throughout Eastern Europe,' and she went on representing the British populist view of foreign affairs in disarmingly simple, not to say simplistic language. I was distressed and so, I noticed, was Hugh Thomas. She was a long way away from any informed analysis of what Europe is now about, what the West German people and opinion-making Germany are like, and what hope resides in a unified Europe. Here was offshore thinking with a vengeance.

The PM observed: 'With the Central European countries re-asserting their independence and all the ancient feuds and territorial disputes resurfacing, we may be going back to the state of affairs preceding the First World War.' Britain, she said, didn't want to end the century facing the same kind of problems with Germany as at the beginning. Some of us doubted whether this was a realistic view. Hugh said that the surest way of going back to a pre-1914 sort of situation is to let the Germans feel that their allies, especially the British and French, are now intent on frustrating unification – something we repeatedly gave our word and our signatures to help them to achieve. The German desire for unity is not necessarily a desire for a renewed nationalism, he said. A united Germany would be smaller than Germany was in 1938; the German birthrate is declining. Self-determination, I added, was guaranteed under Principle Eight of the Helsinki Agreement. Ignoring that would surely be a prescription for trouble. Hitlerism, I said, was in large part a reaction to the Versailles Treaty, and we don't want to create conditions reminiscent of that.

There was a sharp division of views round the table. The PM was visibly shocked to see that some of us did not share either her concept of the 'national interest', or her suspicion that Germany was bound to become a dangerous power again. She was in top gear, friendly but combative, with 'steam coming out of both ears' as Charles Powell once described her to me. Christian names were being used. Geoffrey Howe, on the other hand, was low-key, self-effacing, thoughtful. He spoke little but to the point and highly intelligently. Almost bashfully, he was keeping his eyes on the table. I doubt whether he enjoyed the PM's dominance and strident language, but he showed no surprise. A gentleman to his fingertips.

MT was, of course, the focus of the entire discussion, but there was, alas, also a lot of cross-chat between neighbours. This is a form of dialogue I intensely dislike because it tends to be horribly bitty and inconsequential. This time, however, some of it proved rewarding. Brian Griffiths wanted to know what I thought about Gorbachev's chances of survival, the situation in Hungary, and whether the multi-party system would work. Griffiths said Sir Percy Cradock (the prime minister's foreign policy adviser at No. 10) rated Gorbachev's chances of staying in his job no higher than fifty-fifty. Did I agree with that? I said I did: indeed I rated them no higher and probably even quite a bit lower. I said several American scholars felt Gorbachev didn't have more than a 25 per cent chance of survival, given the fact that the *perestroika* process had been brought into disrepute and had virtually fizzled out. Nikolai Ryzhkov's[1] recent economic report was proof of that. I said all this was dangerous because if Gorbachev fell, there might arise a coalition of hardliners, generals and admirals who would all want to repress the republics. That might lead to civil war and rock the boat of Europe.

1. Soviet prime minister.

Griffiths then asked about German reunification. I said I was a bit reluctant to spell out what David and I had already said over drinks because the prime minister was rather horrified. We were, I said, probably in a minority of three, counting in Hugh Thomas. Griffiths leaned over and said in a hushed voice: 'Not at all, *you* are in the majority.'

'What do you mean?'

'There is only one minority voice around this table and that is a *minority* of *one*,' he said pointedly; 'and that minority is over there' – looking at the prime minister. I was utterly surprised. Griffiths knew the state of the game in No. 10 better than anyone else. If he thought the prime minister was isolated among her colleagues and advisers on Europe and the unification of Germany, it must be so.

Brian Griffiths then asked how I felt about the personalities of Imre Pozsgay[1] and Miklós Németh.[2] He said he rather liked Pozsgay, an agreeable man, he thought, but very much an ideas' man and a poetic kind of a character; whereas Németh, the Hungarian prime minister, was more of a manager who gets things done. I tentatively shared his judgement which, I understand, is also that of the PM. We then went into the Hungarian Democratic Forum's chances of coming out on top at the elections. He was wondering whether this was a predominantly Christian-Democratic sort of a party; was it Catholic or partly Protestant? I tried to explain the background to Hungarian Populism in the 1920s, 1930s and 1940s, how it had been defined by the Protestant stream in Hungarian thinking, and how and why the present Forum inherited many of the characteristics of the peasant-socialist Village-Explorers' 'ideology' between the wars.

The PM's next concern was British productivity, our high imports, insufficient exports and balance of payment difficulties; and she repeatedly claimed that the two Germanies were 'corporatist' states and therefore had an unfair advantage over Britain. Her mind

---

1. Head of the Hungarian Popular Front; member of the Communist Party.
2. Prime minister of the Hungarian People's Republic, 1988–89; Politburo member, 1987–88.

works in terms of a profound economic rivalry with Germany reminiscent of the conflict of power interests before the First World War. Then as now, she seemed to be saying, German economic power was a threat to British industrial interests and self-esteem. What the PM does not see and will not admit is that in the 1980s West Germany and Britain are no longer in the same economic league, and haven't been for some time.

I find the PM's sentiments narrow-gauged in the extreme. No sooner did Soviet power hit the rocks than she and her friends returned, like recidivists, to the scenes of old mischief. They are in search of a new enemy. Almost half a century of a very different world seems to have passed them by without making an impression. They'd be happiest if they could put the clock back to Edwardian days. I'm saddened by this beyond measure.

There followed observations around the table about the non-availability of British-made goods in the shops (in the mêlée it was hard to make out who was saying what). We wondered whether the British were hard-working enough (we know the answer to that!); why the Pakistanis, like the Jews earlier in the century, kept their stores open late into the night and were actually trying to *serve* customers when the ordinary English shopkeepers didn't and weren't. I said that one of the puzzling things about life in Britain in the 1980s was the inefficiency and disorganization of *private* business despite the encouragement it was receiving from Thatcherism. Many private stores didn't keep their eyes on the ball any more than the nationalized companies, and I listed examples: shoe stores that didn't cater for different widths or colours; Marks and Spencer, which would not stock swimwear in the winter or school uniforms in the spring. Chain stores, I said, were forever running out of stock despite computerization, and woe betide if an item had to be ordered. We all produced our pet horror stories. The PM defended none of this. Indeed she was angry, adding a few of her own. 'I usually do my shopping at Sainsbury's, where you get good things cheaply and there is a vast choice, but the small trader just can't afford to keep big stocks,' she explained.

MT was worried about both British performance and British prestige. Why do we import chipboards when these are not high-technology goods? Why bricks and mortar and cement when all these things are made at home? Is our quality inferior, and if it is, why? A range of anecdotes was produced about shops that stock Japanese screwdrivers, German food-mixers, Italian refrigerators, Singapore bulbs – about repair-men who don't keep appointments, bills sent to the wrong address, the long saga of British Rail, and other choice details of life in Britain at a time of peace and relative affluence. Why so much sloppiness and lack of work-discipline? Why? Why?

I will now record something I would have said to the PM very privately had there been an opportunity. But I didn't and couldn't at this lunch, not even among friends. The plain truth is that Margaret Thatcher is in many respects too good for Britain – un-British when seen against the record and mentality of this country in the late twentieth century. She is cut out to be the leader of a nation with the thrift and work ethic of Japan, Germany, Switzerland, Taiwan, perhaps even the US, where her vision, resolve and free-market enthusiasm would produce lasting results. But today the English are not like that – though perhaps the Scots are and once upon a time the English were. The English of our time are short-distance money-makers, satisfied with very small improvements, reluctant to make long-term investments in plant or research, slow to respond to incentives, mentally at odds with the ethos of industrial civilization, frequently feckless and always frivolous. MT, to play on the satirical words of Bertolt Brecht,[1] deserves a more responsive nation. She is cut out to be a wartime leader. History has given her a mini-war in which she shone. Mercifully, she has been denied a large one. But in the deeper recesses of her mind, she regards many of a prime minister's activities in peace as psychological dress-rehearsals for glory to be attained on the field of battle.

I was then asked to summarize my experiences in Poland, where

---

1. 'Would it not be simpler, if the government dissolved the people and elected another?' From the poem 'The Solution' (Die Lösung).

I had just spent a week. I pointed out that the danger of border disputes reopening in Central and Eastern Europe was exaggerated. National animosities in the area, whilst still in existence, were no longer a menace to the peace of Europe. The rabid kind of nationalisms that governed the European scene in 1914 had shrunk to minority problems which affected mainly Transylvania and were unlikely to take the form of warlike action between states. However, the breakup of Yugoslavia and a full Soviet collapse would be a very different matter. These might radiate trouble for the whole of Europe. Both seemed imminent.

As far as economic reconstruction was concerned, there was (I said) one worrying element that eluded our remedies: communist egalitarianism had left deep marks on the people of Central and Eastern Europe. The man in the street, whilst rejecting socialism, nevertheless insisted on a cradle-to-the-grave type of social protection and a risk-free economic order. Private enterprise was suspect, especially in Russia. The PM heartily agreed. 'Yes, George has now spoken a great truth.' (I must say, this is no great truth. Everyone recognizes the dangers of egalitarianism, even the reform-communists did, starting with the 'Prague Spring' of 1968.) She was deploring the fact that in Poland the communist bureaucracy had made such terrible inroads into the economy that even private farming was in a parlous state. The Poles, she said, were unable to produce enough meat and vegetables. Although the Polish peasants were hard-working, their productivity was low because they had been denied tractors, machinery, fertilizers, she said. In the event, I couldn't make a proper presentation of my views on Eastern Europe. The PM was interrupting, then others cut in, but I did have a chance to speak a dozen or so sentences more or less coherently in a few short minutes. Others round the table were even less fortunate.

Brian Griffiths asked me about Lech Wałęsa. What did I make of him? I said I had met him at his union headquarters in Gdansk, then again at a Radio Free Europe celebration in Washington. Whilst I felt he was a genial man with wonderful stories to tell, a real tub-thumper, a marvellous rogue and an engaging demagogue, there was also a wilful, dictatorial streak in him which was bound to come out sooner or later. I related how Wałeşa had told me that at some stage he might run for the presidency, and that I had heard it said in Poland that the reason why he did not mind the powers that were then being gradually centralized in the hands of General Jaruzelski[1] and his office was that he, Wałeşa, was hoping to inherit those powers one day as president. Indeed, one of his personal assistants has already been assigned a post of high rank in Jaruzelski's office as a trouble-shooter. Griffiths and John Whittingdale expressed surprise: 'All who have met him tell us that they were very taken with Wałeşa; he is said to be a man of charm and fighting spirit combined with moderation.' 'Yes,' I said, 'he is a man of great charm but he is also a man who could become a tyrant,' and I mentioned that only a couple of days ago Wałeşa suggested, without consultation with his colleagues or Solidarity leaders in the government, that Parliament should suspend its legislative work and delegate its powers to a temporary committee. This would control the business of the nation. The reason he gave was the economic emergency. Here, I said, was an indication that Wałeşa's democratic credentials left a lot to be desired.

The prime minister had Hugh Thomas sitting next to her. He tried to make a number of points about the benefits of unification enlarging on the virtues of increased cross-fertilization in European culture, the power potential of a wealthy united Europe, and how the future was full of economic promise in a vast integrated market. He said the division of Germany was something forced upon the world by Stalin; the coming together of the two Germanies was a triumph of the West over communism – a victory for all who, like she herself, resisted Sovietism when it was unfashionable to do so. It was also a victory for the Germany of Bach, Beethoven, Goethe and Schiller and other writers and thinkers without whom European culture was unimaginable.

---

1. Wojciech Jaruzelski, president of the Polish People's Republic, head of state, 1985–90.

But the PM was dismissive. 'Don't you realize what's happening? I've read my history but you as an academic don't seem to understand,' and she went on using words which I thought were impolite, even hurtful. Every now and then, talking to Hugh Thomas, she seems to be resorting to language (although it may well be the language of long familiarity) that I have not heard her use with other people. Charles Janson[1] told me that he, too, had seen the prime minister handling Hugh scathingly and talking to him with less than the respect he so richly deserves. This, as I say, may well be due to a long friendship, but I wonder why she does it quite so publicly. In private, she is said to be no kinder to certain colleagues in the government.

Lunch went on for more than two hours. It had the character of a mainly good-mannered fisticuffs. The PM was all rage – then all smiles – hitting highs and lows on the Richter scale in rapid succession; here was turbulent territory one had to approach with caution.

I was hoping there would be a chance for me to talk about the 'boat people' (the forced deportation from Hong Kong of the first batch of Vietnamese). I hold strong views about this and I was not going to hide them. We were breaking faith with thousands of refugees from communism – and our libertarian professions. But the discussion never got round to Hong Kong or the Vietnamese problem. This was a pity, but it did save us more anger. Hugh had told me on the phone that he held equally strong views on the issue but thought the PM would disagree. After lunch I discovered that others shared what Hugh and I felt and were opposed to the deportations. I only hope these forcible expulsions are going to stop. Before going to Downing Street yesterday, I read that the Pope had spoken out and so had Dr Robert Runcie.[2] The public outcry is great by now, and perhaps it doesn't matter too much that none of us had the presence of mind to draw this topic into the conversation. All the same, I feel I dismally failed to do what I ought to have done. Not

---

1. Writer and Soviet/Russian specialist.
2. Archbishop of Canterbury, 1980–91.

long ago I forwarded from Hong Kong a threatened Vietnamese refugee's heart-rending letter to Lane Kirkland's[1] Czech-born wife Irena – a refugee commissioner of sorts at the UN; I know the Kirklands fairly well, but never received a reply.

Towards the end of our lunch the PM made a short speech by way of a valediction: the Centre's work is extremely important, she stressed, because it provides the government with long-term thinking; we should go on banging away at privatization, the reform of education, the promotion of self-reliance and so on.

My general impression is that the PM is in the grips of an attack of 'dogmatism'. She has been in power now for ten years; power does go to the head, even of so intelligent a lady as Margaret Thatcher, whom we always supported and still support. But she is now becoming a symbol of a faded imperial consciousness and of an anti-Europeanism which is unrepresentative of the electorate, even the Tory electorate. Surely this is going to breed trouble for her as prime minister because most of her Cabinet, too, is opposed to her European policies.

As we broke up (Geoffrey Howe made the first move; he said he had an appointment) and were heading for the door, the PM turned back for a moment and, pointing at David, Ronnie Halstead and me, said: 'I wonder if you're still sound? *Are* you sound?' This was unpleasing. Was she joking? We'll never know. A pretty chilling way of leaving her lunch table.

Hugh Thomas, Oliver Knox and I were walking together in torrential rain trying to catch a taxi. Hugh said he had never seen MT quite so pugnacious and xenophobic. I agreed. Hugh was upset; he said he would write to her.

I had been quite prepared, and so had Hugh, for a combative lunch, but it turned out to be much more heated than we had expected. If allied governments knew just how narrow-minded, and in many ways xenophobic, MT has become, they would be even more disturbed than they are already. This is sad. We've been trying

---

1. President of the American AFL–CIO trades union organizations.

to reason her into a more constructive attitude to European unification, but after yesterday's lunch I feel our efforts have been wasted. She seems determined to stick to the antiquated context in which she prefers to see the problems of Europe, and I feel nothing will deflect her from it.

I must add a word here about British technological education. This came up because Charles Tidbury said he was anxious to improve the technical standards of engineers. Why do we not have higher standards of engineering? I ventured to say (à la Koestler)[1] that we have to improve the prestige of technological colleges and the social standing of engineers. We must stop thinking about them as 'nuts and bolts men', as the public still does, and I mentioned that abroad, in Zurich, Berlin, and all over the US, technological colleges enjoy the same respect as the old universities. While everyone heartily concurred, it was asked: how is this to be done, and how do we change public attitudes to work, discipline, cleanliness? The PM seemed extremely worried about this, as well she might. Alas, to be worried after ten years in office is not enough.

At one point I suggested that she might consider launching a campaign (if that was the right word) for a nationwide moral–cultural regeneration, with herself heading it. Wouldn't it be useful, I said, if she made half a dozen appearances on TV in the form of fireside chats so as to bring it home to the public that certain deeper attitudes are at the bottom of Britain's national under-performance, and suggesting ways of raising standards? She gave a rather muted answer: 'Yes, we ought to do so many things, but there are urgent priorities we must tackle first,' and the idea was left hanging in the air.

I believe that moral and psychological regeneration should be our politicians' number one task. Britain's ineptitude in many domains of our industrial civilization is the root cause of our economic and social decline. The country is not performing because the country is not gripped by the spirit of the modern age. This is a long story. I

---

1. The reference is to *Suicide of a Nation?*, a special issue of *Encounter* magazine, guest-edited and partly written by Arthur Koestler, London, July 1963.

referred in our discussion to Correlli Barnett's analysis,[1] and I also
mentioned Martin J. Wiener's book[2] with its parallel thesis: British
cultural prejudices of the nineteenth century caused Britain to be
left behind in the industrial race, in technological sophistication, and
so on. There was no time to discuss any of this in detail, but several
points were briefly touched upon. Everyone expressed unease,
quoting examples from Japan, Germany, Holland and elsewhere to
show that catching up with our competitors was long overdue.

The PM is extremely well informed about virtually every topic,
even Hungarian ones. As I was giving my short report on the East,
Ron Halstead interjected: 'How does this egalitarianism you're talking about express itself in practice?' I said that in Russia the economist Nikolai Shmelev[3] recently gave evidence that private businesses,
even cooperatives, were so thoroughly distrusted by the public that
in quite a few cases they were burnt down. 'What about Hungary;
does the same spirit prevail there?' Ron went on.

I said, no, Hungary had a different tradition. Hungarians were
not steeped in the customs of the nineteenth-century Russian *mir*
(the egalitarian peasant collective), hence in Hungary, even under
Kádár, cooperative and private farming flourished. The PM butted
in: 'Ah, but this is not quite so. I had Prime Minister Németh here
the other day and he told me about a Hungarian farmer who had
built his own silo but had it promptly vandalized by the neighbours.
So even in Hungary it can happen.'

I said, 'With respect, Prime Minister Németh clearly has a more
detailed knowledge of all this than I have, but I would insist that
there is, on the whole, no popular opposition to private enterprise in
Hungary, whereas in Russia there is.'

I am recording this merely to show that the PM misses nothing.

---

1. *The Audit of War: The Illusion and Reality of Britain as a Great Nation*,
London 1986.

2. *English Culture and the Decline of the Industrial Spirit, 1850–1980*, Cambridge, 1981.

3. Soviet reform economist.

She is blessed with a superb computer in her skull with near-perfect recall.

All in all, this was a significant if not a strictly speaking enjoyable occasion. The PM's bitterness at a time of fresh hope was jarring. Yet, despite the heat generated, it was a good-natured occasion – stimulating, laced with banter and much laughter. MT herself stood back from the jocular strain in her guests' conversation. She is a serious lady, uncomfortable with flippancy and hostile to time-wasting pleasantries. I greatly respect her for that. Statesmen – and stateswomen – should have a sense of irony but no sense of humour, and if they do have a sense of humour, they should take good care to hide it from public view. In a country as frivolous as this one, MT's gravitas is a huge national asset.

21 December 1989

True to his word, Hugh Thomas wrote to the PM to express his feelings about some of the things we had heard her say on Germany. He sent me a copy.

Dec. 19, 1989

Dear Prime Minister,

Thank you very much for lunch yesterday.

I was surprised by your mood. Surely the Eastern European counter-revolutions – for of course that is what they are – are splendid proof that the human spirit cannot be crushed – a confirmation that the Soviet Empire there depended on tanks, not attachment to the ideology. The fact that these changes have been so far as we know carried through without bloodshed suggests a degree of maturity amongst the peoples concerned which augurs well for the future. Of course there are anxieties: the survival of a vast Soviet military arsenal and risks of various sorts in the Soviet Union herself among them. But all things considered, the present state of Europe surely gives grounds for optimism not pessimism; after all the Soviet threat, and the threat of Communism, about which you yourself in the past have spoken so eloquently, has, at the least, greatly diminished. Isn't that the main thing? And as

a result are we not in a more favourable moment than at any other time
in our lifetimes?

You spoke very warily of Germany and I don't suppose anything
that I could say could change your judgement. BUT I would say, nevertheless, that a desire for re-unification cannot be surprising and should
not have been a surprise. We have often declared ourselves theoretically
in favour. Even so, it is not certain that all East Germans want it. If it
happened, their method of association would only be confederal. A new
German entity could with skill be fitted into the European Community
in a way which might meet some of our anxieties. There are Germans
themselves who recognize the existence of other people's worries about
German unity. German desires for unity are not self-evidently desires
for revived nationalism. The German birth-rate is in decline and the
sum of the two Germanies would be a smaller country than Germany
was in 1938 by a quarter and a third smaller than in 1910. Finally,
efforts to prevent German unification could cause real German resentment without being effective. It is possible that the real problems of the
future – and of course there will be some – will be quite new: for
example Muslim fundamentalism in France and Britain supported by
Libya or Iran.

Please forgive me if I write too bluntly and thank you again very
much for lunch.

Yours ever,

Hugh

Happy Christmas!

CHAPTER 8

The Chequers Seminar
on Germany

Political forecasting based on 'national character' or the record of 'national behaviour' is notoriously fallible and discouraged by scholarship. It also tends to be condescending. Yet, that is what was broadly required of us when we met at Chequers, on 24 March 1990, to advise the prime minister on 'the German question'.

Having experienced the force of Margaret Thatcher's populist generalizations at the Centre for Policy Studies lunch with her in December 1989, I was apprehensive that, though the cast might be different, the same broad-brush approach would prevail. She would expect us to offer scholarly confirmation of what she had always known 'in her bones' to be the truth about Germany and the German people. It was, I feared, the seal of intellectual respectability she was after as she was coming up to one of the great crossroads of European history – the revision of the results of the First as well as of the Second World War. Raw instinct and raw national interest were to be formulated in the language of disinterested enquiry. It was an unattractive prospect. At the end of such rationalizations lay loaded judgements and international mischief. Raising 'the German question' – like raising 'the Jewish question' – always struck me as a sign of inadequacy in those raising them.

It was, therefore, with some reluctance that I went to the Chequers seminar; but curiosity got the better of me. The dramatic implosion of the Soviet system and empire, followed by what was clearly to be the realignment of the whole of Central and Eastern Europe, were events I was now given a chance to watch from close quarters and offer advice about. My own *métier* was on the agenda; it would have been remiss of me not to be present.

My personal views about the weight of 'national character' in the successive activities of men were stated in a colloquy I conducted with an old and trusted friend, Hugh Seton-Watson, in 1978. Germany and Russia were our theme, and I gently provoked him into saying what, in fact, coincides with my own considered opinions.

'The German past is made up of a number of formative elements. The paintings of Dürer, the music of Bach, the achievements of Frederick Barbarossa and the semi-barbarian culture which Tacitus found beyond the Rhine when he wrote his *Germania* have all gone to shape German culture. Hitler is only one element in that picture. Let us remember that in the mid-nineteenth century (that is, not very long ago) the image which the rest of the world had of the Germans was that of a pleasant, hopelessly inefficient, mild lot of people with whom one could spend hours talking philosophy and drinking good wine ...

'There are highly discreditable elements in every nation's past – the Scots were, right up to the seventeenth century, a barbarous, savage and murderous race who committed the most appalling crimes against one another as well as their enemies. The creation of the modern French nation by the conquest of the French south from the thirteenth century onwards was one of the most brutal chain of events in recorded history ... Yet it would be quite wrong to infer, and nobody does infer, that Scots, or Germans, or Frenchmen are history's natural barbarians or that they possess any other unalterable characteristics – good, bad or indifferent.

'We are, all of us, involuntary legatees of our national past, and we must be conscious of our national past – but we are not *slaves* to our national past.'[1]

It was with such ideas in mind that I approached, with some trepidation, the prime minister's seminar.[2]

---

1. Hugh Seton-Watson and G. R. Urban, 'The Fall of Multinational Empires in our Time', in G. R. Urban, *Communist Reformation*, London, 1979, pp. 319–21.

2. For six years, the ethics of confidentiality dissuaded me from publishing my diary entries about the Chequers seminar. But as the other private participants have all told their story, and Baroness Thatcher omits mentioning the meeting in *The Downing Street Years*, I feel no longer bound by confidentiality. To have a full account on the record of what really transpired is especially important in the light of misrepresentations that appeared in the media and questions asked in Parliament.

Diary

Sunday 25 March 1990

An all-day seminar yesterday on Germany, at Chequers, at the invitation of the prime minister.

Those present were Margaret Thatcher and Douglas Hurd, foreign secretary; from the United States, two distinguished historians: Gordon Craig and Fritz Stern; on our side Lord Dacre of Glanton (Hugh Trevor-Roper), Timothy Garton Ash and Norman Stone from Oxford, and myself. The prime minister was assisted by Charles Powell, her foreign policy adviser and factotum in No. 10 Downing Street.

I was introduced by MT to those I hadn't met as 'the man who runs several important radio stations', but I quickly assured her that that had never been the case, much less was it true today, and that I had stopped running Radio Free Europe in 1986. But, clearly, I still figure in her mind as one who knows all about international broadcasting, opinion-making, the contest of ideas and so on. She was too kind.

Nine years ago, on 24 January 1981, I had been sipping tea in the same place with another group, shortly before Mrs Thatcher's first visit to the newly elected Ronald Reagan. Our task then was to help her with ideas to shape her relationship with the new president. That was the last group session I attended at Chequers (I saw her privately, though, on other occasions). But those were more confident days.

I drifted aside for a while with Douglas Hurd. We chatted about the Romanian/Hungarian situation. I told him I was appalled by the events in Transylvania and had little doubt that behind the beating of Hungarians in the centre of Tîrgu Mures were the old but now sidelined Securitate[1] interests, aided by the Iron Guard from outside Romania. He appeared greatly interested, especially when I told him

---

1. Communist Romania's security police.

I had just returned from a large Anglo-Romanian conference in Bucharest, which had been organized by Jessica Douglas-Home's Eminescu Trust. Despite the bloodshed, there had been no de-communization, I said.

This is Mrs Thatcher's third term, and she is under formidable attack, especially on account of the Community Charge (poll tax). Conservative defeat at the Mid-Staffordshire by-election[1] doesn't help. MT looked rather tired and quite a bit older than she had done even a few weeks ago. I did see her briefly at the Centre for Policy Studies annual general meeting last week where she made a re-soundingly successful speech and was as fresh, as convincing and charming as ever. But even then she wasn't at her best, showing signs of being at the receiving end of much stick and intense carping that are now daily coming her way from all quarters: the press, much of the parliamentary party, Conservative 'supporters' and so on.

Fortunately, yesterday's lunch and seminar were exclusively devoted to foreign affairs. Not a word was spoken during our formal sessions, or informally, about the rising challenge to her position, which she has so far headed off with her usual panache. I admire her ability to stand up to hardship; she is seldom rattled. Most people would have gone under in the face of a tenth of the vitriol that has been used on her by her own side, but she has immense reserves of energy and a great ability to protect and project her personality.

At lunch I was seated between Hugh Trevor-Roper on my right and Timothy Garton Ash on my left; next to Trevor-Roper: the prime minister; on her right Fritz Stern, Norman Stone, Gordon Craig; further to my left, next to Timothy Garton Ash, Douglas Hurd and Charles Powell. It was a small lunch, ten people all told including Denis Thatcher, who was seated facing Margaret Thatcher

---

1. On 22 March 1990, with a 21 per cent swing, Labour overturned a Conservative majority of 14,654, gaining the seat for Sylvia Heal with a majority of 9,449.

in the middle. He said nothing memorable within my earshot. Of the six 'advisers' I was the only non-historian, if historians are those who are members of university faculties – which raises the tricky question of who is 'lay' and who is 'professional' in the eyes of the history trade union. Arnold Toynbee and I discussed this in 1971 in a broadcast conversation,[1] and he observed wryly that in the eyes of British purists neither Gibbon, nor Acton nor Macaulay – nor indeed he himself – counted as 'professional'.

As the first course was being served, MT, always the good head-mistress, said, 'Well, I have long experience of these discussion-lunches; there is usually confusion as to who talks to whom, and what's being said, so I have a suggestion to make to you. During the first part of lunch let's talk left, and during the second part let's talk right; that way we can avoid cross-chat and chaos.' Now this was, for me, a novel approach to taking a meal. There is, under the surface, a Prussian sergeant-major of the nineteenth century lurking in the PM's soul. We received MTs orders with jokes, and general hilarity followed. Like disciplined soldiers, however, we started talking left. Timothy Garton Ash drew up his chair, 'All right then, we're going to talk to each other as commanded – a bearable fate.'

Garton Ash was wondering whether Romania was ripe for demo-cracy and to what extent the Romanian events reflected the survival of the Communist Party in disguise. Tim is an excellent analyst; he is young and has already made a name for himself. I can see in him a future R. W. Seton-Watson or a politician of the first water. He is rational, can think on his feet, and his heart is very much in the right place – with one or two exceptions: he made misjudgements about Nicaragua and has a soft streak in him when it comes to the Third World, but on Eastern Europe he is sound and has written some excellent stuff. In Munich in 1984 I offered him a top job at Radio Free Europe as my deputy. Luckily for him, he declined.

After the main course, I spoke, as ordered, to Hugh Trevor-Roper

1. Arnold J. Toynbee and G. R. Urban, *Toynbee on Toynbee*, New York, 1974, pp. 28–36.

while MT chatted with Gordon Craig but, despite the arrangements, no common topic emerged. I thought the 'left turn' didn't really agree with us, and the 'right-turn' wasn't doing much better. Some symbolism there?

Trevor-Roper and I discussed our recent joint publication in the journal *Encounter*[1] which, as I told him, had drawn some interesting reactions. He said he too had a couple of letters, some of them critical. One had come from the German writer Johannes Gross, who liked just about nothing in our article. I said that one telling letter I had received with an enclosure had come from my friend Leszek Kolakowski, the distinguished philosopher and fellow of All Souls College. It had to do with a bit in our conversation where I asked: How would our leaders behave if a post-Hitlerian Euro-Nazi, a Nazi 'with a human face', were in power today as a result of a German victory in 1945? Would Mrs Thatcher, Reagan and Bush befriend him in the same sort of way as they befriend Gorbachev? To this Trevor-Roper answered in *Encounter*, 'Oh yes, most likely they would.' Leszek Kolakowski's letter picked up that statement. He said: 'You posed a hypothetical question. I had posed the same sort of question in the *New York Times* in May 1975 in a sarcastic editorial to mark thirty years of peace under a victorious but de-Hitlerized, Euro-Nazi Germany.' He enclosed what he had written. He had, indeed, preempted my question and Trevor-Roper's response by fifteen years. Kolakowski's point was that our spineless politicians would have been just as willing to appease and do business with the Euro-Nazis as they were in fact doing business with the *détente*-minded Brezhnev and other Soviet 'liberals'.

Apropos of correspondence, Hugh said, 'One letter I had was from Charles Janson. Do you know him?' I said I did, and we fell to talking about Charles's outstanding abilities and how they'd been left somewhat unexploited because of his marriage to the charming Elizabeth, Countess of Sutherland. We said that Charles's position in the aristocracy deprived him of the need to engage in intellectual

---

1. 'Aftermaths of Empire', *Encounter*, London, December 1989.

pursuits for his bread and butter, and when a man of his great gifts is given too much freedom to relax, spending a lot of his time in Scotland and Elba, then he is less likely to produce the gold that is potentially in him. We both said Charles was a brilliant, incisive but rather unfulfilled man. Trevor-Roper knew him in Oxford. Then I told him about the Alexander Zinoviev factor and Charles's great attachment to Zinoviev and his wife Olga.[1]

After lunch the group went upstairs, where a seminar room had been laid out. I was rather surprised to see how formal it all looked. Around an oval-shaped table spaces had been set out by name in a very cabinet-like manner. MT sat behind 'Prime Minister', next to her was 'The Rt. Hon. Douglas Hurd, MP, PC', 'Lord Dacre' and then the rest of us – professors, doctors and misters.

MT took the chair and opened the discussion. We would, she said, first talk about the historical background of Germany and the reliability of Germany as a future partner in Europe: to what extent was Germany, through its freshly won or prospective economic might, likely to become a politically over-powerful and perhaps even aggressive factor? And she made no secret of her conviction that Germany was indeed historically a dangerous power, not only because of the First and Second World Wars, but because of the sheer size of her population, the diligence and discipline of her people, the unreliability (as she called it) of the German character, the likelihood of Germany embracing another 'mission' in Europe and so on. In other words, it was fairly obvious from the moment she began speaking that her gut reactions were anti-German. This wasn't of course news to me because at our CPS lunch with her at 10 Downing Street on 18 December, 1989, she made her feelings about Germany depressingly clear in the face of objections from various people at the table, including Hugh Thomas and myself. On that

---

1. Alexander Zinoviev, Soviet-Russian dissident philosopher and mathematician, author of *Yawning Heights*, *The Reality of Communism* and other works. Janson believed at the time that Zinoviev was in the possession of a more reliable method for deciphering the Soviet system than were Western scholars.

occasion, too, she sounded emotional and in some ways surprisingly simple-minded. So, yesterday at Chequers, I expected more of the same and that's what we got. But the PM did not harangue us. She appeared to be genuinely anxious to find out what all these 'distinguished' observers and historians had to tell her.

My impression is that she rather expected our group to endorse her anti-Teutonic preconceptions, and that she probably invited the two Americans with that idea especially in mind. She could have had no illusions about my own or Norman Stone's views on the subject, as Norman had made it repeatedly clear in various newspapers that he believed the German Federal Republic was a force for the good which would have to play a very prominent part in the future of Europe. I had said similar things in *Encounter* and repeatedly to MT herself in my conversations with her, notably that we ought to embrace Germany as an ally; that we must not disappoint the hopes of Europe by being too negative, raking over the past at a time when we had to look to the future after the miraculous delivery of Eastern Europe; that we must produce ideas and inspiration of our own. When I saw her privately at No. 10 in 1984, urging her to assume a leadership role in European unification, I spoke about Germany in a similar vein and put my thoughts on paper at her suggestion.

Trevor-Roper, too, was on record, in our *Encounter* piece, and apparently in a speech he had made in the House of Lords recently (which incidentally the PM had read but I hadn't – she's a remarkable lady; her appetite for information seems insatiable) to the same effect; so MT could have been in no doubt about the attitudes of Trevor-Roper, Stone and myself – three out of six. I should imagine she assumed that the Americans and perhaps Garton Ash would take a more sceptical view. Not so.

There was surprise in the air when, starting with Gordon Craig, followed by Trevor-Roper and then Fritz Stern, we all came up with analyses I would roughly summarize like this: while the 'German mind' (if there is such a thing) is spiritually and intellectually not always easy to fathom because of Western ignorance and the peculiarities of German history and political culture, the Federal Republic has given a splendid account of its ability to run not only a democratic system, but a liberal democratic system at that, with a strong element of social responsibility and institutional guarantees built into it. These could not be easily circumvented by a future extremist party or a dictator. Our general conclusion was that whilst a certain amount of caution is always very much in order in politics, this is a Germany 'worthy' of British trust (I found the condescending tone quite intolerable); a Germany with which Britain must closely cooperate; a Germany which is a very important economic partner; and even if a reunited Germany were eventually to flex its muscle because of its wealth, such economic muscle-flexing would speed up overall European reconstruction and would, in any case, be held in balance by the continuing existence of NATO and a more intense development of the European Community. The latter, we said, were German desires even more than they were British or French. Qualifications were made.

The prime minister said she thought the German minorities in Eastern and Central Europe were, or could once again become, a problem of the 'fifth column' sort – that these groups, such as the Germans remaining in Silesia and Romania, might give us the same kind of trouble Hitler created by playing on German grievances vis-à-vis Czechoslovakia, in Danzig, and so on. I pointed out that this was not so: the German minorities were desperate to move out of Russia and Central Europe. Reinforcing my view, Garton Ash said the remaining German diaspora had but one desire – to give up their status as diaspora; far from wanting to generate a German irredenta, their hope was to move to friendlier pastures in the Federal Republic lock, stock and barrel. I added that the ethnic Germans in Transylvania and Russia had an interesting history in that they had arrived there not as conquerors but as border guards and 'development aid'. They had been *invited* in, granted local autonomy, tax incentives and other privileges by Géza II, Maria Theresa and Catherine the Great. The settlers' job was to transfer 'know-how' in the arts, crafts and industry. Today, Gorbachev was rehabilitating the Volga Germans and was most reluctant to part with them. There were suggestions, I said, that Kaliningrad, the former Königsberg, should serve as a special economic zone for them, because the Russian leaders felt that these dedicated citizens could turn Kaliningrad into a great port and a prosperous city again. Similar plans were under discussion for the Volga region itself. MT appeared to have no knowledge of any of this, but, of course, she couldn't be expected to.

Listening to us the PM remained diplomatic but unconvinced, firing questions at us to express her deep doubts. We answered with courtesy and in impeccably scholarly terms. Procedurally, of course, we all deferred to her because she was in the chair, she was the prime minister, and our hostess. We didn't interrupt her inter-jections, which were many, although she frequently cut into our words – but that again is a prime minister's privilege. There were no rows or even 'words'. But stage by stage, it emerged clearly enough that, collectively, we had very different views from those she was entertaining and especially those she had, damagingly enough, put on the record since the fall of the Berlin wall.

It was fairly obvious that, in his bones, the foreign secretary was on our side of the argument. This chimes in with my reading of his character and his background, and also with what I had heard from Hugh Thomas. They had been colleagues and friends in Cambridge. Hugh had told me a couple of times that Hurd is really a convinced European and that he should be a beneficial influence on Margaret Thatcher's instinctive anti-Europeanism and anti-Teutonic feelings. This, I thought, proved to be the case. I could sense how he was trying to go along with us, without openly saying so. His whole demeanour and the way he was nodding when certain arguments were produced gave me the impression that he was in disagreement with MT's unwavering scepticism. Before lunch, I said to him, standing some distance away from the rest of the group: 'Well, it seems we are going to have quite a bit of an argument because some of our views on Germany are clearly not in line with those of the prime minister.' Hurd answered rather quietly: 'Don't let that worry you. We have already worked on her and she is changing. Speak your mind absolutely freely because that's what we're here for, and she would like to hear your and everyone else's criticisms if that is what they are going to be.' And, of course, we did just that.

At the end of a long day (and I am now jumping ahead a bit; the discussion ended around five and we stayed on for another hour or so until about 6.30) MT said: 'Very well, very well, I am out-numbered round this table. I promise you that I shall be sweet to the Germans, sweet to Helmut when he comes next week, but I shall not be defeated. I shall be sweet to him but I will uphold my principles.' So it remains to be seen what effect, if any, this discussion will have on her.

As we were walking out to get into our cars, Norman Stone, Timothy Garton Ash and I huddled together. It was remarkable, we said, that our consensus should have developed quite independently. Neither the Americans nor the four of us from this country had any idea who was going to attend the seminar; much less could we coordinate our views. We were not in any way close friends – yet we all came to the same sort of conclusion: the PM's 'instincts' were extremely wide of the mark. Craig and Stern said they were thrilled by the invitation. No American president since Kennedy would have had either the intellectual curiosity to enlist the views of scholars, or the ability to debate with them as an equal. They were too right. MT is a great lady even when she is dead wrong.

Our seminar coincided with a day of high drama in Lithuania. It was a sign of Margaret Thatcher's power of concentration and mastery of detail that, looking at her watch, she suddenly said that at five o'clock this afternoon, British Time, which was, she pointed out, seven in Lithuania, the Soviet ultimatum for the return of Lithuanian deserters from the Red Army would expire and this could end in high drama. If the deserters were not to surrender at the appointed places and were then arrested by Soviet officers, and if they then offered resistance, there might be a very nasty punch-up which might start a whole sequence of violence in Lithuania with unforeseeable consequences.

This led us to talk about what help, if any, we ought to be giving the Lithuanians. And although she could sense that some of us were anxious that Western help of some sort, certainly moral support and international backing of a more than symbolic kind, should be given, she was adamant that this could not be done because it might hurt Gorbachev and even result in his fall. And to keep Gorbachev in the saddle was, she said, very much an American and British political priority, because without Gorbachev none of the recent Eastern European developments could have occurred, and with his fall a dangerous situation might arise. I support her in this – up to a point. Gorbachev is, perhaps unwittingly, destroying the Soviet system. We couldn't have done better had the CIA appointed its own man to 'reform' the USSR. I once jokingly suggested to John O'Sullivan over dinner in New York that Gorbachev *was* a Western agent and urged him to write it up by way of testing the reaction in Moscow!

We all recognized that there was a dilemma here, or rather that all options were undesirable. If we abandoned Lithuania to its fate completely, and if Gorbachev insisted on reasserting Soviet power there, and if he did so using armed force and other nasty means of pressure – and this is what he has been doing in the last several days – then his credit in the West would vanish. Both *détente* and *perestroika* would be facing very hard times. But if he did nothing, he would inevitably come face to face with the disintegration of the Soviet empire.

I ventured to point out that Britain wasn't a free agent in the matter; the British choice would be much influenced by what the Americans did, and my experience of the US was that the Americans had a very strong Baltic lobby which would sooner or later press the president and the State Department into taking much firmer action, or at least taking up a firmer rhetoric on Lithuanian and the other Baltic countries' independence than has been the case so far. If that happened Britain would have to follow suit. The group recognized that this might occur, but of course we had no certainty that it would, although since our meeting yesterday Vice-President Quayle has already uttered more robust words on the Baltics than Bush did.

All this was debated for a while in the sense that the Soviet empire was indeed in a state of rapid fragmentation and that any talk about writing off NATO, on the grounds that there was no obvious need for it, was premature. I'm not sure whether the PM liked my un-subtle hint at our satellite status *vis-à-vis* America.

'Fragmentation' led us to the Romanian–Hungarian situation. Later on, privately, the fighting between the Hungarian Székely minority and the Romanians in Transylvania, especially in Tîrgu Mures, was discussed, and I might as well make a note here that, when Norman Stone and I talked to the foreign secretary off the seminar table, we tried to impress it on him that the violence in Transylvania was the work of the Romanian extreme nationalists, egged on probably by the former Securitate and the Vatra[1] people, both being aided from abroad by remnants of the Iron Guard. Later, standing around the fireplace, we made similar points to Margaret Thatcher. She felt that the National Salvation Front in Romania was indeed a bequest from the communist regime, and that reforms of a very drastic kind would have to take place before we could support the present or any future leadership.

Earlier I had drawn the foreign secretary's attention to the fact that on 20 May free elections were scheduled to take place in Romania, and by all the indications we had seen it was quite likely that for the first time in history (apart from Chile) a communist government of sorts would be elected through the free vote of the people. This would be perverse and a blow to our cherished notion that Eastern Europe was waiting to be liberated, but if it did happen we would have to think very hard about what policy to pursue towards Romania and how we might give effect to the idea of self-determination as written into principle VIII of the Helsinki Agreement.[2]

---

1. Vatra Romaneasca, Romanian ultra-nationalist organization.

2. The forecast proved accurate. The National Salvation Front, manned by leading former communists, received over 60 per cent of the vote in both the presidential and parliamentary elections. Ion Iliescu became president and Petre Roman prime minister.

Margaret Thatcher pointed out that self-determination was a dubious prescription because it failed to take care of the extraordinarily complicated ethnic and religious structure of the Soviet Union and much of Eastern Europe. (Did she have Ireland in mind?) This was hardly news for those of us who had spent years studying the problems of nationalities in the Habsburg Empire; the work of the Versailles peace conference; the dismemberment of Austria-Hungary, and the rise of the successor states. But MT presented her doubts about the applicability of self-determination under current conditions as some revelation freshly sprung from the head of Zeus. Nevertheless, she was, of course, right and Woodrow Wilson had been wrong. Politely, we concurred.

It was depressing to see that Margaret Thatcher's attitude to the whole problem of Germany was so much that of a novice, despite the learned books she had ostentatiously piled up in front of her on the seminar table. She didn't hide her cordial dislike of all things German (forgetting, it seemed, the Teutonic descent of the English nation, of the English language and of the royal family), aggravated by her distaste for the personality of Helmut Kohl, whom she saw not at all as a fellow-Conservative or a Christian Democrat, but as a German deeply mired in provincialism.[1] The contrast between herself as a visionary stateswoman with a world-view, and Kohl the wurst-eating, corpulent, plodding Teuton, has a long history in MT's imagination. Kohl's effectiveness in Europe was, she thought, due purely to the money in his pocket and the respect money commanded in the world (could this be wrong for a true Thatcherite?). And she was wondering how long it would be before German economic might were translated into political power – in which case she felt Germany would have won the Second World War, because what

---

1. Chancellor Kohl returned the prime minister's dislike. Horst Teltschik notes in his diary (29 March 1990): 'This evening the Chancellor flew to Cambridge for the Königswinter Conference ... He was greeted at Cambridge airport by Margaret Thatcher. At Kohl's request, they drove separately to St. Catherine's College. He is still under the influence of his anger over her comments on German policy in this week's *Spiegel*.' Teltschik, p. 188.

'the Germans' could not attain by force of arms 'the Germans' would now be attaining by economic clout. I was appalled. Were these the views of a responsible prime minister?

She also made plain her affinity with Gorbachev. She told us after the meeting how she had received him 'on the very spot where we are now standing' (hallowed ground), in front of the fireplace, early in the game, before he was elected general secretary; and she pointed out, looking rather pleased with herself, 'Well, those were days when Chernenko was on his last legs, there was a gap in the Soviet leadership, and we were all looking for the next man to take power. There was Romanov[1] whom no one took terribly seriously, although he was in the running, and there was Gorbachev. I was talent-spotting in the Soviet leadership, and that's how Gorbachev came to visit me here in Chequers. I immediately hit it off with him and that's when I coined the phrase "we can do business with him". My whole relationship with Gorbachev was and is based on that first meeting.'

MT's extravagant admiration of the Soviet leader struck me as most significant, especially when juxtaposed with the fact that Germany is, deep down in her mind, still Britain's real foe. Russia, although not to be trusted either, is a distant factor, a barbarian factor, but also a balancing factor. You've still got to keep your powder dry against Russia (she seemed to be saying), and you still have to do everything to secure British survival in an unforeseeable conflict; but in her subconscious thinking I nevertheless detected a hankering for the verities of the Second World War, if not the First. No emotion can equal a real old hatred.

I reflected aloud on some of this at our plenary session: was it, I said, really a useful exercise for us in Britain to go on reliving the glories of the Second and First World Wars, rather than preparing ourselves for constructive action in the given situation? This was a time of enormous relief, of a great triumph and new horizons:

---

1. Grigory Romanov, powerful first secretary of the Leningrad Communist Party.

a totalitarian system with worldwide ambitions had gone down; a system we had feared, against which we had armed ourselves and spent much of our time and treasure to keep at bay, was no more. Why didn't we now take a more generous view? Why didn't we make a bonfire of ill-fated balance-of-power ideas and plan for the future of the whole of Europe?

MT kept coming back, in response to this kind of argument (for some of the others were taking a similar line), with words like: 'But can we trust them?' She would accept that the Federal Republic was a responsible, democratic state in its financial and economic policies, helpful and humane all round, but could the Germans be *trusted*? What about those Prussians and Saxons who were now joining West Germany but had had no experience, since 1933, of any political system other than Nazism and Stalinism? How did we know what they might do and think; and wouldn't we therefore be giving hostages to fortune if we vested too much confidence in an enlarged Germany?

I detected in all this the survivals of a deep sense of national rivalry with imperial Germany. MT's distrust harked back to the build-up of the Kaiser's sea-power, and to British alarm at seeing things happening in technology and world trade that threatened to beat Britain at its own game. Long memories don't help. The current phase in the Anglo-German psychodrama bodes ill for British participation in Europe, although I think MT is realistic enough to see that, like it or not, Britain will soon have to play a more positive part than it has been playing so far, or else leave the Community.

Time and again the prime minister stressed that NATO must not be allowed to disintegrate. One of us said the situation in Russia and general uncertainty in Eastern Europe did indeed make NATO's continuing existence absolutely essential, and we discussed the possibility of the fall of Gorbachev; a much harsher nationalistic (if reduced) Russia playing an important and possibly aggressive role in the world; how the Americans were unwilling to keep forces in Germany without nuclear cover; and whether intercontinental missiles in Britain could qualify as 'nuclear cover' now that it has become virtually impossible to modernise short-range nuclear weapons in Germany because of the resistance of German public opinion. MT repeatedly expressed her astonishment at the strength of neutralistic trends in Germany. She resented German resistance to low-flying exercises, Allied tank manoeuvres, and the like. She was worried that German public opinion might, whether under an SPD government or a coalition, push a united Germany into *de facto* neutrality even if, on paper, Germany remained part of NATO. And she made no secret of her conviction that American and other Allied forces must stay on German soil – in effect, as occupation forces and as double insurance that Germany would not jump ship.

In response to all this, Trevor-Roper and the two Americans observed, using different forms of words, that, of course, there could be no *absolute* assurance about the future. There never could in history. But we could say that the record of the Federal Republic had been very good. German attitudes, both private and public, had fundamentally changed since 1945. The teaching of history in German schools was now so thoroughly reformed that we need not fear a return of extreme nationalism, much less any kind of Nazi mentality. Trevor-Roper gave a graphic description of how he had convinced himself that this was indeed so. He'd attended an Auschwitz war crimes trial in Frankfurt, and was delighted to see how the young generation were totally untouched by the spirit of Nazism and were appalled by what they heard at the trial. This, he said, convinced him that there had indeed been a sea-change in German thinking. Others around the table quoted examples to the same effect.

At the risk of being repetitive: I'm not at all sure that MT was swayed by any of this, because she went on and on telling us, 'Yes, yes, but you can't *trust* them.' She has the historical experiences of the last war and the First World War so deeply embedded in her soul that no evidence or rational argument will change her image of Germany. She thinks she represents British opinion; and although we tried to suggest to her that, certainly the younger generation (i.e. people under forty) were far from being unanimously behind her in this – that, indeed, they were supporting the unification of Germany and of Europe – we didn't seem to be having any visible impact.[1]

I said at one stage that, just two or three weeks ago, the BBC and the *Guardian* ran a joint opinion poll in the Soviet Union about German reunification with quite unexpected results: the majority of those polled – two-thirds or more – supported German unification. 'How do we explain that?' I asked the PM. 'Why do the Russians support unification and why do you think Britain and France should be more suspicious than the Russians who bore the brunt of the war?'

MT said, 'Ah, well, I was myself surprised by that result, but there is an explanation. The Russians have a peculiar mentality. They argue: "Yes, but we *defeated* the Germans; why should we be frightened of them?" She thought this was a perverted argument but that's how the Russians felt. The Russians, she said, thought they were secure because of their tremendous victory over Germany – so secure that any new German menace struck them as a fantasy. Like her, I felt this Russian argument to be plain foolish, but I'm not convinced such an argument really exists. The Russians, in my view, support unification because Germany is geographically close, and they hope to benefit from a grateful and prosperous Germany. There is also an old Russo-German cultural link – a kind of mutual admiration nexus – which needs to be taken into account.

I said: 'Aren't we uttering collective judgements, assuming and saying that the Germans are guilty "in the seed", as it were, *collectively* guilty; and doesn't this run counter to all our professions of liberal democracy and individual responsibility? We keep saying that the Germans are to be suspected because of Hitler, but we don't say all Frenchmen are suspect because of Napoleon, or all Russians because of Ivan the Terrible, or all Jews because of the genocidal things Joshua committed in Canaan a few thousand years ago. Isn't

---

1. This was Lord Dacre's impression too. 'As for Mrs T— I think that, having heard us all, she will be of the same opinion still!' he was to write to me from his home in Didcot on 28 March 1990.

there a touch of racism in all this – the very sin we condemn in the Nazis – as well as a lack of Christian forgiveness?'

The PM wouldn't have that. She interjected, 'Yes, but in the cases of Napoleon and Ivan the people didn't have a free vote. Hitler, however, was *voted* into power.' Stone cut in to correct her, and I reinforced what he was saying. We told her (although not precisely in these words) that, before their 'Seizure of Power' on 30 January 1933, the Nazis never attained anything like a majority either at national or local elections. Running against Hindenburg for the presidency in March 1932, Hitler's share of the vote was only 30.1 per cent against Hindenburg's 49.6 per cent, and when the election had to be repeated in April, because Hindenburg had fallen short of an absolute majority, Hindenburg won with an absolute majority of 53 per cent as against Hitler's 36.7 per cent. Even at the 5 March 1933 Reichstag elections, conducted under a reign of terror following the Reichstag fire, the Nazis won only 43.9 per cent of the vote, and had to face a large though disunited and demoralized opposition. But MT held on to the 'Hitler was elected' argument regardless, ascribing in effect a kind of collective guilt and unalterable national character to the Germans because of this imaginary popular vote for Hitler in a free election.

Not only did the PM display bias against Germany, but she was also taking an odd pride in doing so. Throughout the day she let it be known that she was speaking for the robust, no-nonsense instincts of the great British public, and no continental politician was going to tell her what to think or what to do. She was not going to tolerate German 'domination' or any undue political influence flowing from economic power. She was resentful that the French, the Belgians, the Dutch and others were, as she thought, succumbing to this influence. They were over-impressed by Germany's economic might and unwilling to stand up to her.

The PM, I noticed, is also very conscious of what she thinks were personal slights and insults on the part of various Germans on the diplomatic circuit. She didn't bring up the famous and possibly apocryphal Salzburg gateaux-eating episode with Helmut Kohl as

protagonist,[1] but she told us repeatedly how at some EEC meeting
or other the Germans were supposed to have said, 'We're now paying
the piper, so we're calling the tune.' And although she thought
German officials were trying to appear politically low-key and cooperative, one could, she claimed, already see a certain great-power
swagger in their step. They had all the money and they wouldn't let
you forget it. Then came Kohl's ten-point schedule for unification,
which he had not cleared with the British or the Americans or the
French. This greatly upset MT. And she has a great fund of other
stories of various pinpricks that UK officials are said to have suffered
at the hands of German officials. So I sensed in MT's words a
hypersensitivity bordering on paranoia which can only lead to more
trouble, more misunderstandings and disenchantment in and with
Europe. For no good reason I can put my finger on, MT is on the
warpath on the Teutonic front, and I don't think this can benefit
Britain.

In our first session, the two Americans and Trevor-Roper were
our principal speakers, the rest of us playing minor parts. But I did
have a chance to say: 'I've just come back from visits to East Europe
– Romania, Hungary, Poland, East Germany – and my principal
impression is that here is a continent anxious to return to its status
as a single civilization. We once called it Christendom. But the East–
Central European parts of this once single body are mortally sick.
They are plague-ridden as a result of forty-odd years of Communist
rule. Somehow or other they have to be cured and reclaimed. The
rest of Europe, too, is at risk as long as the Eastern parts are in a
state of terminal decay. Reclamation and reconstruction, moreover,
have to be quick and effective, and the country that can do all that
with the best hope of success is Germany. And if, at the end of the

---

1. Helmut Kohl, while on his annual holiday near Salzburg, is said to have
cut short a meeting with the prime minister, quoting as his excuse an earlier
arrangement in his calendar. But later in the day, MT, while walking along one
of Salzburg's fashionable thoroughfares, saw the chancellor in a *Konditorei* enjoying, without company, a large Austrian cream gateau. She is said to have been
greatly offended.

day, reclamation were to bestow increased economic influence on a united German state, I for one would accept that as a reasonable price to pay for restoring the health of our entire continent. Who else would or could do it? We? The Americans? The French? The alternative is destabilization.'

MT's response was: 'Ah, what you are saying is "suck up to rich uncle, suck up to rich uncle, so that he is then nice to you." No, no.' A bit later in the debate Norman Stone put in his oar: 'Well, I do agree with George on this question of reclaiming Central and Eastern Europe, because it is in an appalling state. It is sick, it has to be brought back into our community, and if the Germans are the ones to do it best and quickest, well, so be it, we can live with that, but we must not have a Europe that is half-rich, half-poor; half-stable, half-destabilized.' I doubt whether we managed to dent MT's preconceptions, but we certainly made a strong pitch.

Timothy Garton Ash provided indirect supporting fire. Some people in the West may think, he said, that when the Germans expand into Eastern Europe they are laying their hands on cheap labour, cheap land and cheap everything, and that this will give their economy an even greater lead than it already has and amount to a form of Third World neo-colonial exploitation. The problem, however, is that the nations of Eastern Europe are in such dire straits that they are actually *asking* to be exploited, *asking* for German (or any) investment and capitalism. And he added wryly: it is a proverbial truth by now in the Third World that there is only one thing worse than neo-colonial exploitation: non-exploitation. The same goes for Eastern Europe. The PM smiled but I thought she was not amused.

After the meeting, over drinks, we touched on Hong Kong and China. MT said the only communist country (apart from Korea) that really resisted radical reform was China, but she was hopeful that somehow or other the Chinese communists, too, could be eventually softened up or undermined before the Sino-British Treaty expired and Hong Kong was integrated into China in 1997. Looking at me she said, 'Well, of course, one of our problems is that we haven't been making the kind of propaganda effort in our broadcasts to the Chinese as we have towards Russia and Eastern Europe. Why do the Japanese not do it? Are they doing it?' She turned to Hurd for an answer. 'No, the Japanese are very thin on the ground as far as radio propaganda is concerned,' he said, adding with a smile, 'but even if they did make a greater effort they wouldn't be the most credible or popular source for the Chinese to listen to.' Hurd was right.

'Well, George, you're the man who knows all about intellectual warfare. Why don't you people go into Chinese broadcasting and make it more effective? It might have some influence.' I said the Chinese service of the Voice of America was highly effective, and so was the BBC's, but not enough was being done. And I added, jokingly, 'Prime Minister, if you gave the BBC, Bush House, shall we say £20 million extra money to mount a round-the-clock broadcasting effort to China, it *might* have some loosening-up influence. I am a little doubtful, but it might.' She said, 'Not at all, the BBC have plenty of money, they've got all the money they can use. They should use the money they have more effectively.' But I could see that Douglas Hurd was glad that I'd said what I had because the Foreign Office has an interest in beefing up the BBC's Chinese broadcasts and, who knows, MT's enthusiasm for an expanding effort may surface in some memorandum or other in the coming weeks and perhaps lead to increased broadcasting hours and a better signal.

MT was in the mood for covering enormous ground (she usually is). The focal point of the seminar was, of course, MT herself, exactly as she had been at our No. 10 Downing Street lunch before Christmas. There, despite the presence of Sir Geoffrey Howe, the deputy prime minister, MT was clearly, forcefully, almost offensively, in command. This time, the part of demure understudy was being played by Douglas Hurd, standing or sitting there like a well-disciplined prefect, too nice and too much of a gentleman to make waves, but obviously pained and unhappy. As soon as MT started interrupting he would stop and yield to her, as indeed we all did. But for a man who is foreign secretary to be quite so abashed and to be quite so ready to withhold opinion surprised me. It was, for me at least, abundantly clear who was in charge of policy-making, and I'm not at all sure whether this is a good thing in matters of European policy either for Britain or Europe. More Cabinet responsibility and Cabinet decision-making are now called for. The PM resents Kohl because he is successful and a Teuton to boot; she resents Delors[1] because he is a socialist and a French 'centralizer'; she resents the Benelux leaders because they won't annoy Germany. Where is this taking Britain?

Fritz Stern made a good point emphasizing the strength of West German institutions. He said the parliamentary system, the independence of the courts, of local government, and the autonomy of the Länder were so powerfully entrenched that it would take a long chain of disasters to shake them; there were also the European institutions, which were strong and well respected. The Federal Republic was solid, responsible and predictable as a partner and major influence. He said that: of course, only a prolonged economic crisis could ultimately test the staying-power of German democracy, but he was confident that Germany would meet that test, too.

One of the most powerful arguments of the day was put forward by Lord Dacre – an argument which is common currency for most of us in the field, but coming from him, it made a special impression. I had used it myself talking to MT on earlier occasions. Hugh said he could not quite understand the government's fears of a free and united Germany. After the war, the Allied intention, the Anglo-American intention, was to have a single Germany, a single Germany in freedom, and it was wholly against that intention that, because of the unyielding nature of Stalinism, Germany had to be split into two states. And he quoted chapter and verse to show that Churchill's intention, Attlee's intention and the Americans' and NATO's intention was a free and united Germany. Why then, he said, was the government so horrified now that the original post-war aim of Allied

---

1. Jaques Delors, president of the Commission of the European Communities, 1985–94.

policy was being suddenly achieved – without war, without blood-shed, without a crisis of any sort, purely because the communist antagonist has given up? We have a free and united Germany presented to us on a plate. Why our apprehension? How can we now possibly wish to put off or negate unification? We should rejoice, because we've won.

The prime minister was a little taken aback. There were muttered voices of approval around the table, with Fritz Stern, however, saying yes, yes, we all wanted to have a single Germany in freedom, but it must be admitted that, when such things were being first said, every-one assumed that a united Germany would be a Germany of rubble and disorganization; whereas now the materialization of our post-war aim of a united Germany means a free and democratic Germany that is also domestically prosperous and economically powerful. Hence some people's apprehensions. He was saying this, he went on, not to justify the PM's fears, but simply by way of adding a reminder that the context in which our earlier attitudes had been formed was different.

While all this was being said, the foreign secretary was subdued and mostly silent. He came into the discussion periodically but only briefly and mostly to support or qualify some point made on our side. He said repeatedly that the only policy issue that should con-cern us was the translatability of Germany's economic power into political power and how that power would be used; that was the real question. But he was, in my judgement, visibly unhappy about the prime minister's emotional tone and her reluctance to go along with some of our reasoning. Margaret Thatcher was certainly assertive and refractory. Before anyone could finish an argument she would butt in and say something assertive like: 'Ah well, but not when you are talking to *Germans*. They will always be the same,' or 'How could they have done it? This was a civilized, highly cultured nation, Goethe and Beethoven being among their cultural heroes; how could they have incinerated people in Auschwitz?' etc. All of which is, of course, very true and no one would wish to deny the Nazis' guilt, least of all the Germans themselves.

Gordon Craig pointed out that one couldn't make any criticism of the Nazi past that had not been made by the Germans themselves a thousand times over. Some of the breast-beating was almost embarrassing. But I think the prime minister was not quite aware of this. She seemed to have no knowledge of the strength of the anti-Nazi element in German politics, or of the power of self-incrimination in the whole of post-war German political culture. This point, as I say, was strongly made by several of us, especially Gordon Craig, but also by Lord Dacre, none of which, however, helped, as I think, to make a decisive impression.

At one point, the 'insensitivity' of German politicians came up for discussion. We went back to Bismarck and looked at the opinions and feelings of Germany's neighbours. Craig thought the Germans were no great masters in the refinements of diplomacy and tended, over the last hundred years or so, to use language and pursue policies that rode roughshod over the feelings and interests of the Poles, the Dutch, the French and the Belgians. Stern added: 'The Germans were such a go-ahead nation under the Kaiser, they were so rapidly advancing in terms of science, industry, culture and music that they had the best possible chance to occupy a proud place among nations. In 1914, however, the Kaiser and German militarism ruined that chance, pushing the world into the deepest catastrophe.' So, said Stern, Germany squandered one set of golden opportunities, and this squandering of opportunities continued with Hitler into the Second World War which, he implied, was the second act of a single drama.

Now, he went on, Germany had another chance, which history seldom grants to nations. Because of the astonishing collapse of communism, and especially the delivery of East Germany, Germany has been given an unexpected fresh opening. It was, he said, most unlikely that today's democratic and enlightened Germany would repeat the follies of its predecessors, squandering once again Germany's chance to rise to preeminence through its civilian virtues. The Federal Republic, he noted, was the most successful state and polity yet experienced in recent German history. The German people and their leaders would not jeopardize it.

At which point Margaret Thatcher observed rather testily: 'Well, well, do you then want Germany to be a great leading nation, do you?' Gordon Craig cut in with words to the effect that we couldn't raise objections to a democratic and liberal Germany, set up by ourselves, trying to play a distinguished role in the world. We couldn't possibly wish a democratic Germany not to rise to its opportunities. A free and united Germany had been our stated aim in all our post-war policies. It was now about to happen – unless Germany were gripped by some extraordinary and unforeseeable distemper which he, Craig, would find hard to imagine.

I could sense that the prime minister was not happy with any of these observations. They did imply that Stern and Craig thought that indeed, it would have been better for the world if the Kaiser's Germany had not provoked war but attained preeminence among nations by peaceful means. By the same token, they appeared to be implying that it would be a good thing now if a fully democratic Germany used its present opportunity to attain peacefully some of those things which were perhaps due to a nation of Germany's size, energy and cultural attainments.

Throughout these exchanges, it became more and more obvious that MT's status in her own eyes as the repository of truth and rectitude had grown enormously since my first meetings with her in 1981 and 1982. She has become a lady of overweening self-confidence and self-importance, particularly, I should imagine, in her dealings with her inferiors in the bureaucracy and her colleagues in the cabinet; and there are signs that this is being increasingly resented. I wonder how long it will be before opposition within the party erupts (it is already there, as a matter of fact) and threatens her leadership.

I still support MT because of her courageous domestic record, her leadership in the Falklands crisis, her intellectual curiosity and charm (and not least, I must confess, because she honoured me repeatedly with her confidence), but my doubts about the wisdom of some of her foreign policies have increased in recent months and the seminar yesterday did nothing to allay them. We can only pray and hope that she will be guided, under the influence of Geoffrey Howe and Douglas Hurd, by less irrational ideas than she is now, but that she will not do so willingly I am pretty certain.

As we were about to leave, with drinks in our hands, the PM repeated, 'I'm taking to heart what you've all said; Chancellor Kohl is coming; we are going to have a long session in Cambridge,[1] and there is the EEC special summit coming up in Dublin;[2] I'll see what I can do.'

I suggested once again, this time rather jokingly as befitted the hour: 'Why don't you, Prime Minister, make a sweeping gesture and redesign our entire relationship with Germany, giving our European policies a fresh start, because we are, after all, in the possession of very good news?' There were, I said, many highly positive elements in the history of Anglo-German relations we could build on – not least the fact that the most successful features of the present German system, e.g. the organization of the media, the unions, the idea of co-determination in industry, the Works' Councils, and much else, were of British design under the occupation regime. 'Well, now, I can't do any of that,' she said, 'you are going too far. That's what *you* might want to do, but I have to represent what people *feel*, and I don't think they would feel that way. We've got to be reasonable, but we must keep our powder dry,' and so on. Norman Stone and Timothy Garton Ash nodded in support of my slightly bantering plea.

Monday 26 March 1990

I will go on about Chequers. We talked repeatedly about the need to keep NATO alive and the difficulties of so doing in the light of German impatience with nuclear weapons and forward defence. Having discussed this for a while I said that in the past our Soviet 'friends' had a way of solving such problems for us. Whenever *détente*

---

1. At the 20th Anglo-German 'Königswinter conference' on 29 March 1990.
2. 28 April 1990.

reached a point where we thought we could relax our guard, the Russians would do something outrageous to put everyone on the alert again. 'The disastrous state of the Soviet Union could propel the Russian leaders into doing something rather rash again, perhaps even today, in Lithuania.' It was indeed one of our immediate concerns to examine what the Russians might do next: whether they would try to arrest the Lithuanian deserters, suppress the government, prevent the Lithuanians from putting up border posts on the Russian frontier, forestall the organization of a civil guard, whatever. I am recording these notes forty-eight hours after the seminar and it would appear that some of the measures I feared were being taken as we spoke. In the meantime, the Lithuanian government, expecting the worst, named its Washington representative as its plenipotentiary with presidential powers in case the Soviets decided to suppress the free government in Vilnius.

For me, none of this came as a surprise. I related over drinks what I had told Marju Lauristin, then head of the Estonian People's Front, in the course of a discussion in September 1988: 'It would not take spectacular military measures – much less an invasion of Estonia – for the Russians to be able to suppress you. They have their forces on your territory; they could, in a single night, take over the whole National Independence Movement by occupying the radio station, the television station, the airport, other public buildings, and arresting perhaps three dozen leaders such as yourself. And unless the Estonian people were ready to fight on the spot, and fight overwhelming odds, I can't see how they could succeed.' Measures of that kind, I said to the seminar, are now being taken or threatened in the whole Baltic area.

The prime minister said, 'Of course, all this has been considered; we realize there is unrest in the Soviet Union, even civil war is not excluded; the Red Army itself is profoundly disunited and rival factions may emerge.' And we mentioned Christopher Donnelly[1]

---

1. Head of the Soviet Studies' Research Centre, Royal Military Academy, Sandhurst; later adviser to the secretary-general of NATO.

and Peter Frank's[1] recent analysis at NATO headquarters, which had been leaked to the press and predicted the end of *perestroika* and a profound crisis, possibly reaching civil-war proportions. 'This is a danger that does preoccupy us a great deal,' she went on; 'but although trouble in Russia would keep NATO alive, our dreams and hopes would be ended because we did think a better world was on the horizon, that the Soviet system was profoundly changing, and that the Soviet Union might turn into a democracy like Czecho-slovakia and Hungary. Now, if civil war or even just permanent unrest broke out, all those great promises of '89 and early '90 would be shattered.'

We fell to talking about Gorbachev's future. I asked whether she thought the new powers Gorbachev had taken as president were a good thing for the Soviet people, or for us. Gorbachev, I said, was assuming powers far in excess of those Stalin himself had possessed; these could lead to a complete personal despotism either in his hands or in the hands of his successors. I could, I said, envisage the rise of future Stalins or future nationalist/fascist/communist leaders who might, having inherited Gorbachev's powers, rule the country with the knout,[2] becoming a menace to their own people as well as to the outside world.

MT pooh-poohed the idea. 'Oh, we don't have to worry about that. As long as Gorbachev is president I have no fear at all that he would abuse his powers. He's not that sort of a man. We know Gorbachev – he stood right there in front of the fireplace when I first met him ...' I have related the rest of this story. I got some support again from Norman Stone and Tim Garton Ash, both of whom said that indeed Gorbachev's powers were quite formidable and might lend themselves to abuse; but again, MT wouldn't have it. 'Ah, but we can't afford to look that far ahead in history. We should cross our bridges as we come to them and not worry about the distant future.' At the moment, she said, she was satisfied that

---

1. Professor of Russian history at the University of Essex.
2. Whip formerly used in Russia as an instrument of punishment.

Gorbachev did need fresh powers and that he would make cautious use of them. If dictatorial power had been Gorbachev's ambition, he would have been content with his position as party general secretary. That is all Stalin had, and look at the use *he* made of it, she said. This is, incidentally, Gorbachev's own answer to people questioning the expansion of his powers as president.

Here was further evidence that MT's attitude to the world's politicians is now highly personalized. So much subjectivism in a prime minister is dangerous, and although I believe that in a critical situation she would not allow herself to be entirely swayed by personal predilections, I find her uncritical self-confidence worrying.

Thursday 29 March 1990

This morning, five days after our Chequers meeting, I collected a registered envelope from the Post Office. It had come from Charles Powell, dated 19 March, and could not be delivered in my absence (I had been away in Liechtenstein). In it he gave us an outline of the topics the PM wanted to see discussed at Chequers. His agenda was, to say the least, unusual. Most of the questions were loaded and virtually answered themselves. I'm inserting them here for the record.

Basically the prime minister's objective is to use our knowledge and experience of Germany's past to help shape our policy towards Germany and Europe for the future. She will want to tap the wisdom of each individual participant for this. I suggest, therefore, that we should devote the first half of the afternoon to Germany's past and the lessons to be learned from it: and the second half to wider questions about Germany's future role in Europe, and what changes this may require in our diplomacy.

For the *first part* of the discussion, the following are some of the questions which we might consider (although the list is neither comprehensive nor exclusive):

— what does history tell us about the character and behaviour of the German-speaking people of Europe? Are there enduring national characteristics?

— have the Germans changed in the last 40 years (or 80 or 150 years), either as a result of some mutation in their national character or because of changes in their external environment?

— what is the key to German economic success? Is it something deep in their character and psyche, a natural sense of discipline and order? Or is it 'simply' sound policy?

— what will be the tendency of a united Germany? Despite all protestations to the contrary, will it lurch inevitably and as often in history, towards geographical and territorial dominance? Or will it find satisfaction in the creation of something broader than Germany?

— how strong is the drive to unite all the German-speaking peoples, either within the existing borders of Germany or by extending those borders?

— in the light of history, how can we 'satisfy' the Germans? Is there something *they* want and *we* can give them, which will neutralise their drive to extend their sway, whether politically or territorially?

— how strongly German do the remaining Germanic minorities in Eastern Europe and the Soviet Union feel? Is an ambition to protect them likely to resurface as a factor in German policy?

— will German national ambitions be subsumed in the internationalist appeal of a European Community as they claim? Can the sense of German nationhood be supplanted by the sense of being part of a European nation? Or is this wishful thinking on their – and our – part?

— how deep-rooted is the German mission in Central and Eastern Europe? Is it part of their instinctive and historic restlessness? Or is it merely a current calculation of economic and political advantage?

— can we deduce from history how the Germans as a nation will respond to certain sorts of treatment? Is it better psychologically to 'stand up to Germany'? Or to pursue a friendly approach, based on understanding of their needs and ambitions?

— looking back through history, are there traits in Germany's relations with Britain which have been particularly positive and on which we can try to build in future? Are there some particular aspects of the German character or of German national interests to which we can appeal, to forge a cooperative relationship?

— to what extent do we need to take account of the growing influence of people of Germanic origin in the United States, as a factor affecting American policy towards Europe?

In the *second half* of the discussion, the prime minister would like to range more widely and consider some of the broader consequences of German unification. We might look at some of the following questions:

— one might say that in the past, history was determined largely by the personalities and ambitions of the *rulers* of peoples. In future it may be determined more by the character of the *people* themselves. What will the implications be, given the resurgence of national feeling in Eastern Europe in particular?

— given worries about the dominant influence which a united Germany might exercise, what sort of framework should we build in Europe, into which a united Germany would fit comfortably (for future economic, political and defence cooperation)? Is the European Community sufficient? Or should we look for something wider?

— to what extent should such a framework provide also for the Soviet Union, as the only power in Europe capable in crude terms of balancing a united Germany?

— is there still a use for some of the concepts familiar from history such as spheres of influence, geographical alliances and balance of power? Or should we be looking at something much broader, for instance an 'alliance for democracy' which would stretch from the Atlantic to the Urals and beyond?

— how are we going to cope with the return of national feeling in Eastern Europe, now that events of recent months have shown that forty years of communist oppression failed to suffocate it?

These are just illustrative questions – and formulated by me rather than by the prime minister. But I hope you will find them of some help in preparing your thoughts.

Newsnight on BBC2 has just given sound-bites from MT's and Chancellor Kohl's Cambridge speeches. The differences between her approach and his were striking. Yet our impact on MT's thinking can be detected (as far as I can judge without having seen the texts) from the fact that she spoke about tightening the Helsinki formula and using the forthcoming Helsinki Conference for the creation of a legally binding international agreement, and subsuming German unification under that tighter and more binding international instrument. This was, in fact, suggested by some of us at the Chequers meeting. We didn't work out a tidy formula, but we did say that she might try to carve out of the CSCE[1] process a smaller body to which perhaps only a dozen countries would be invited to belong, and which might then draft a text to serve as a substitute for a German peace treaty. This she appears to have accepted. She insisted, however, on keeping modernized short-range nuclear weapons on German soil. We tried to talk her out of that because we knew it would have absolutely no support in Germany. Kohl's emphasis on the need to embed German unification in the unification of Europe – in political, monetary and even defence unification – was very much at variance with what MT was saying and what is known to be her thinking on unification. The Anglo-German differences are still there. Short of a change of leading actors, they are bound to remain.

Some of my own tentative predictions about Lithuania seem to be coming true. I said at Chequers that the American Congress would be subjected to heavy Baltic pressure urging recognition. This seems to be happening. It started happening last Sunday, and it will go further. At some point the British government, too, will have to take a more robust position than the prime minister has done so far. I am aware of all the reasons why this is difficult to do and may not seem judicious at the moment, but it has never paid in history to take an amoral or less than fully moral position on vital issues such as national independence, self-determination, civic freedom and human rights.

MT told us apropos of Baltic freedom that she and the government had to make strenuous efforts over the last few days to dissuade MPs and especially peers from asking questions in the House about Britain's outwardly inactive attitude to Baltic independence. Under-lining, in these critical days, that Britain had never recognized the Baltic states' incorporation in the USSR would embarrass Gorbachev, she said. Keeping Gorbachev in good working order was her first priority.

---

1. Conference on Security and Cooperation in Europe.

CHAPTER 9

Fallout of the Chequers Seminar

On 15 July 1990, almost four months after our meeting at Chequers, the *Independent on Sunday* published Charles Powell's 'confidential memorandum' on our discussion. It was an astounding document – not so much for what it actually reported (though what it did was in many places inaccurate enough), but for its particular, and unashamedly anti-German, flavour. Here was rich fuel for diplomatic misunderstandings and the perpetuation of national stereotypes.

'We started by talking about the Germans themselves and their characteristics,' Powell minuted. 'Like other nations they had certain characteristics, which you could identify from the past and expect to find in the future. It was easier – and more pertinent to the present discussion – to think of the less happy ones: their insensitivity to the feelings of others (most noticeable in their behaviour over the Polish border), their obsession with themselves, a strong inclination to self-pity, and a longing to be liked. Some even less flattering attributes were also mentioned as an abiding part of the German character: in alphabetical order, *angst*, aggressiveness, assertiveness, bullying, egotism, inferiority complex, sentimentality. Two further aspects of the German character were cited as reasons for concern about the future. First a capacity for excess, to overdo things, to kick over the traces. Second, a tendency to over-estimate their own strengths and capabilities. An example of that, which had influenced much of Germany's subsequent history, was the conviction that their victory over France in 1870 stemmed from a deep moral and cultural superiority rather than – as in fact – a modest advance in military technology.

'To an extent,' Powell went on, 'Soviet and East European interests paralleled those of Western Europe. We wanted Germany to be constrained within a security framework which had the best chance of avoiding a resurgence of German militarism. We wanted a continuing American military presence in Europe as a balance to Germany's power. We would want to see limits, preferably self-imposed through a further CFE[1] agreement, on the size of Germany's armed forces. We would want a renewed self-denying ordinance on acquisition by Germany of nuclear and chemical weapons. We would want to involve the Soviet Union institutionally in discussions of Europe's future security through CSCE, not least because in the long term ... the Soviet Union would be the only European power capable of balancing Germany ... It was pointed out that the more assertive Germany became, the easier it ought to be to construct alliances against Germany on specific issues in the [European] Community.'

The reaction was worldwide and instantaneous. That Powell had 'flavoured the rich soup with a little of his own spice'[2] was one of the more charitable comments to appear in the British press. 'Few member-states of the European Community can ever have disscussed one of their partners in terms like these,' an authority on Germany observed.[3] A leading article in *The Times* said: 'The leaking of a memorandum purporting to give an account of Mrs Thatcher's meeting of academic and other specialists on German history is regrettable ... The damage was compounded by the sensational style in which the Prime Minister's foreign affairs secretary, Charles Powell, chose to record the discussion. The offending list of alleged German traits at the start of the memorandum was of attitudes which the participants were invited to discuss, not endorse ... Mrs Thatcher ... should ... ensure that her aides, if they must put their thoughts on paper, do so accurately and with commonsense. She should also be more discreet in her own views on Anglo-German relations.'[4]

---

1. Conventional Forces in Europe.
2. Timothy Garton Ash in the *Independent*, 17 July 1990.
3. Neal Ascherson, 'Be nice to the Germans, PM told', *Independent on Sunday*, 15 July 1990, p. 1.
4. 18 July 1990.

Diary

20 July 1990

[I cannot conclude this account without saying a word or two about the Powell memorandum leaked to the *Independent on Sunday* on 15 July. Whether the leak is related to the Ridley scandal I cannot tell. Ridley, of course, richly deserved sacking, but MT's own views about Germany are, alas, in no way different from his.]

Charles Powell's version of what was said and concluded at Chequers is an interesting piece of writing, but is very much at odds with what actually happened. I was extremely upset. So, as I soon discovered, were the other British participants.

Both Stone and Garton Ash had misgivings.[1] I immediately rang Powell to enquire whether this was, in fact, his memorandum. He said it was, and when I told him that I could hardly recognize in it what had been said at Chequers or – and especially – the mood of the meeting, he observed: 'I've been taking minutes for a long time but nobody has yet accused me of fabrication or inaccuracy.' I repeated as politely as I could that his account was liable to give rise to serious misunderstandings, and I wondered why we hadn't been shown a draft.

In a BBC *Newsnight* programme on Monday, I made the point publicly too, and so did, in slightly more guarded language, Stone, Stern and Garton Ash. We were weighing our words perhaps rather too carefully out of courtesy to the PM, and because we thought – certainly I thought – that we were under some obligation of confidentiality. So at least Charles Powell advised us when the invitations were made. Clearly, Powell himself didn't feel that the rule applied

---

1. Three years later, in October 1992, in Berlin, Lord Dacre, with whom I was sharing a platform at *Encounter* magazine's closing-down conference, asked me, 'Have you done anything about the way we have been misrepresented in Charles Powell's memorandum? I haven't, but we should. I'm deeply embarrassed when German friends ask me "Do you really hold those views?"' We then decided to think of some effective way of putting the record straight, but have not done so to this day.

to him or his office – if, that is, the leak had come from government quarters. Yet it is difficult to see where else it could have come from.

The episode is most embarrassing. All of us 'advisers' have been dealing with Germany for many years and are known to our German and other continental and American friends to hold views greatly at variance with Charles Powell's summary. I think I'm right in saying that all of us admire the achievements of the Federal Republic; and I have myself been particularly anxious to remove any remaining suspicion between the Federal Republic and its wartime Western opponents. My editorial instructions to Radio Free Europe as its director in 1983–86 are proof enough. In one executive guidance to mark the fortieth anniversary of D-Day, I reminded staff that what the Western leaders were remembering on the Normandy beaches was the defeat not of the German people, but of a despotic and inhuman system of government. Our broadcasters were advised to shape their comments to Eastern Europe accordingly (8 June 1984). To be then tarred with the brush of anti-Germanism is a blow to everything I stand for.

Charles Powell's leaked memorandum is so constructed that while some of the details, when taken in separation, do not always misrepresent what had been spoken or touched on at Chequers, they are nevertheless embedded in a *mélange* that has a deeply anti-German, even racist, flavour and has been so interpreted both in this country and abroad. But even many of the details represent observations I cannot recognize.

I certainly have no recollection of having said or heard at Chequers anything like: 'The more assertive Germany became, the easier it ought to become to construct alliances against it in the EC' (also a headline in the *Independent*).[1] I didn't say 'We wanted a continuing American military presence in Europe as a balance to Germany's power.' I most definitely didn't say 'Soviet and East European interests paralleled those of Western Europe' *vis-à-vis*

---

1. p. 19. The text was followed by a biting comment by Neal Ascherson, 'A raft poled into the sunset by a mad Queen'.

Germany. I most definitely didn't say 'We would want to involve the Soviet Union institutionally in discussions of Europe's future security through the CSCE, not least because in the long term ... the Soviet Union would be the only European power capable of balancing Germany.' The list of things misremembered in the memorandum is a long one. Powell apart, anyone familiar with my career and publications would find it inherently impossible to believe that I would have wanted to bring the Soviet Union into any European settlement directed against Germany. A similar 'repackaging' of the evidence by Radio Free Europe journalists would have sent heads rolling under my stewardship.

Fortunately, in Monday's *Independent* (16 July), Douglas Hurd, too, was quoted as being unhappy about Charles Powell's memory. Under the front-page sub-headline of 'Foreign Secretary repudiates No. 10 think-tank minute', Anthony Bevins, the paper's political editor, reported:

> Questioned on the Chequers meeting yesterday, Mr Hurd said: 'The verdict clearly was [out of that meeting] that it is a fantasy to suppose ... that it is overwhelmingly [likely that it's] a fantasy to suppose ... that we're going to be faced with a new Hitler or a new Gestapo. We could only *dismiss* that as a possibility'.[1]
>
> That statement endorsed the view of some of the experts who also attended the meeting. Yesterday they repudiated the suggestion of 'unease' about future German ambitions expressed in the Powell minute. That minute also spoke of German characteristics, including aggressiveness and bullying, which were not recognized by some of those present.
>
> It said while there were no real worries about the new German generation 'it still had to be asked how a cultured and cultivated nation had allowed itself to be brainwashed into barbarism. If it happened once, could it not happen again?' Mr Powell reported: 'In sum, no one had serious misgivings about the present leaders or political élite of Germany. But what about 10, 15 or 20 years from now? Could some of the unhappy characteristics of the past re-emerge with just as destructive consequences?'

---

1. My emphasis.

It was that suggestion of lingering doubt which was attacked yesterday by some of the participants – who revealed that the minute issued after the meeting bore a striking resemblance to a two-page No. 10 questionnaire circulated by Mr Powell to six British and American experts a week before the Chequers session on March 24.

One of those present, George Urban, described Mr Powell's questions as 'loaded' and the questionnaire as a 'self-fulfilling prophecy'. He said: 'The concerns expressed in it have, in fact, found their way into the summary of the meeting.'

Another participant, who asked not to be named, said: 'I thought that the memorandum contained a good deal of the questions which had been put to us rather than the answers which were given by us.'

In another report, also on the front page, the *Independent* went over the same ground quoting Norman Stone, Timothy Garton Ash and myself (as well as the fourth, unnamed, British participant) as challenging 'the accuracy of the official account of the meeting held by Margaret Thatcher at Chequers'. The coverage was rounded off by an outspoken leader under the title of 'Staggering Condescension':

Even allowing for the likelihood that the Prime Minister and her known prejudices set the tone of the seminar, and that the summary by her private secretary, Charles Powell, may have been tendentious and unfair, it reveals a staggering degree of smugness and condescension towards the country of Bach, Beethoven, Goethe, Schopenhauer, Kant, Willy Brandt and Helmut Schmidt – not to mention hundreds of thousands of Germans who defied Hitler and died for their beliefs.

It is pretty rich for any gathering which includes Margaret Thatcher to accuse an entire nation of insensitivity to the feelings of others, let alone of being obsessed with itself. Neither at home nor abroad is Mrs Thatcher known for her sensitivity ... In few foreign countries is there as genuine interest in other people, and what can be learnt from them, as in Germany – notably among the young. Chauvinism is a French, British, American and Japanese speciality ... .

I must repeat here what I told the *Independent*: a closer look at Powell's memorandum shows one remarkable thing – it is conspicuously in harmony, not with what had transpired at Chequers, but with the themes Powell himself sent us under his own signature as topics the PM wanted to have discussed. They virtually contain their own answers. Also, they are very much in line with the strange things I heard Powell say about Germany at a CPS dinner not so long ago. Remembering his words and, more important, the PM's strident views at our Downing Street lunch last December, I was seriously wondering whether I shouldn't make some excuse for skipping the Chequers seminar. But, then, my commitment to Powell – whose unflinching dedication to MT I respected – and, I admit, curiosity, made me decide otherwise. I came back just in time to make the meeting. On second thoughts, perhaps I shouldn't have.

When all is said and done, Powell's much-quoted account is a piece of special pleading. Unquestionably, the PM – and Powell – were anxious to have confirmation from us of all the things Powell had implied in his questionnaire, but we just didn't oblige. Some of his themes were challenges or moots rather than considered statements a scholarly group could be expected to spend time discussing. Nor have I any recollection of serious thought being given to Powell's by now famous 'characteristics' the Germans are supposed to have: '*Angst*, aggressiveness, assertiveness, bullying, egotism, inferiority complex, sentimentality ... capacity for excess, kicking over the traces', etc. These saloon-bar clichés were simply not discussed and would have been politely dismissed had any attempt been made to subject them to serious consideration. Of course, MT herself is not at all unwilling to talk about the Germans (and other foreigners) in such portmanteau terms, and it may well be that over lunch or tea she did so privately, though not within my earshot. Only last Friday one of her (unnamed) senior colleagues was quoted in the papers as having said: 'Anyone who has attended ministerial meetings with the Prime Minister, as I have, will tell you that if it's not the unspeakable crimes of the German people, it's the perfidy of the French, the idleness of the Mediterraneans, the slit eyes of those to the East, the blackness of those elsewhere, the views of her brother-in-law on his farm in the South of England, or those of the people in the flats of Finchley.'[1]

But to allege, as Powell does, that his puerile list of 'characteristics' was somehow at the centre of our attention at the seminar is preposterous. It wasn't. But once a misrepresentation of this kind has been publicly made, no denials or corrections can undo the damage. Powell may have pleased the PM, but he has done the country, and certainly all of us individually, a disservice.

I seldom agree with Labour foreign policy, but on Tuesday, at Question Time in the House of Commons, Roy Hattersley[2] took MT to task in a way that pleased me. I wish it had been done in a non-adversarial framework by a senior Conservative.

Mr Hattersley: Is the Prime Minister aware that four of the six academic experts who attended her Chequers seminar on Germany have said that Mr Charles Powell's minute of that meeting gave a slanted – that is, anti-German – account of the discussion? Does the Prime Minister agree?

The Prime Minister: No, Mr Speaker.

Mr Hattersley: The whole House, and people in many places and chanceries throughout the world, will be astonished that the Prime Minister has not taken this opportunity to repudiate the more offensive sections of the minute. Four of the experts at the seminar say that the minute was slanted against the Federal German Republic. Everyone in the world now believes that the Prime Minister's private secretary was reflecting not so much the opinions of the experts as the prejudices of the Prime Minister. Why does she not take this opportunity to refute them?

The Prime Minister: I am amazed that the deputy leader of the Labour party chooses his opportunity to question me to use it – [Interruption.]

---

1. Anthony Bevins, *Independent*, 13 July 1990.

2. Deputy leader of the Labour Party; former secretary of state for prices and consumer protection; former shadow home secretary; former shadow chancellor of the exchequer.

Mr Speaker: Order.

The Prime Minister: – chooses to use his opportunity for questioning to attack a civil servant who cannot reply and who has served all Governments with equal integrity. His conclusion on that meeting was highly constructive, as was the meeting itself. There used to be more honour in the House than that.

Mr Hattersley: The Prime Minister's reputation is far too tarnished for her to maintain this haughty stand any longer. Does not she understand that there is a problem with Anglo-German relations and that that problem is the Prime Minister? What we want – and, I believe, what the majority of people want – is an honest statement of the Prime Minister's opinion. Has she the courage to make such a statement to the House and to face cross-examination?

The Prime Minister: Perhaps the Right Hon. Gentleman will read the many speeches and consider the many actions in which we have been staunch allies of Germany in NATO and in which the Germans have been staunch allies of ours in NATO and in the EEC. Germany joined us in stationing Cruise and Pershing at a critical time. We could not say that the Opposition supported that.[1]

---

1. *Hansard*, 17 July 1990, p. 859.

CHAPTER 10

After the Fall

Margaret Thatcher's bitterness in the wake of her fall as party leader and prime minister, followed by her afterlife as an international celebrity, repay study. No other democratically elected and subsequently defeated head of government left office with so little grace, or went on showing himself or herself on the stage of the world with so little modesty. The dedication and single-mindedness that had earned Margaret Thatcher fame and respect while in office were harnessed, after her departure, to the display of frustration and anger. She had been loudly jubilant in her years of success – she was loudly embittered in her afterlife.

Her metamorphosis was quick – it was also very un-English. There was to be no dignified retirement for her – in the mode of Churchill, Attlee, Macmillan or Callaghan – to savour the joys of quiet reflection after a stormy and exceptionally successful public life. Where other defeated or retired leaders chose to crown their careers by withdrawing to the moral high-ground, Margaret Thatcher went on fighting from the wings, unreconciled to the loss of power, second-guessing and subtly interfering with the work of her successors, especially in foreign policy. John Major, her preferred successor, was 'not his own man', she let it be known soon after Major's accession; his government, she indicated, was betraying her policies.

It was a spectacle at odds with Margaret Thatcher's great days as an inspiration of people and a source of radical ideas. What a splendid legacy she would have left behind had she gone quietly after her second term rather than later – had she jumped, and not waited to be pushed, when the party and much of the electorate were still behind her and her hubris on Europe had not yet undermined Tory cohesion and the reputation of Britain in Europe. But the lady's make-up demanded otherwise.

Seen in a larger perspective, Thatcherism was a necessary but an intellectually modest departure. The cult of Margaret Thatcher's personality, especially in the United States, can hardly be ascribed to a 'big idea' or the call of any ideology. Thatcherism was a way of redressing the balance between the state and the individual, a reversion to *laissez-faire* economics and Victorian values – a reversion whose time had come and which proved initially highly successful. But Thatcherism contained no stirring message for Western audiences – nothing to bring people out on the streets or send the television ratings soaring. Yet she was able to do both.

Almost the whole of Margaret Thatcher's charisma in the West arose out of a curious combination of factors psephologists cannot test or sociologists measure: her displays of instinct where the rules of caution normally obtain; her relentless perseverance where compromise is the cachet of approved behaviour; her defiance of established authority, including vested conservative interests, but – above all – her gender.

Her image as a woman of pleasantly orthodox appearance, harbouring explosive ideas and an uncontrolled tongue, brought her greater admiration – and hatred – throughout the Western world than her advocacy of privatization or supply-side economics. Despite her indifference to feminism, her gender was the key to Margaret Thatcher's fame.

She was a woman in a man's world, hence larger than life and louder than a man's voice would carry. Had the same qualities gone into the making of a Harold Wilson or Alec Douglas-Home, the world would hardly have noticed. In her, they became a cause and travelled well for a limited period. At the age of seventy, Lady Thatcher 'reached the fateful condition of being famous for being famous.'[1]

Seeing her again soon after her involuntary resignation promised to be rich in reflection and anger. Charmed lives have a way of exacting cruel penalties.

Diary

19 December 1990

Margaret Thatcher came to lunch at the Centre for Policy Studies. Hugh Thomas was acting as host, with Raymond Carr,[2] Ronald Halstead, Dominic (Chai) Lieven, Oliver Knox, Nils Taube (from

---

1. Hugo Young in the *Guardian*, 23 November 1995.
2. Sir Raymond Carr, historian; warden of St Antony's College, Oxford.

Rothchilds), David Willetts, Ken Minogue, John Hemming (of the Royal Geographic Society) and myself as the rest of the cast. Originally Douglas Hurd was going to be our guest, but he cancelled and Hugh invited MT to do us the honour.

We were meant to be talking about 'The Legacy of Communism after the Fall of the Soviet System' but, predictably, we didn't stick to that elevated topic. Expertise was meant to be supplied by Chai Lieven, Carr, Hugh and myself, but I could sense from the beginning that this was going to be no ordinary lunch but a kind of lamentation-cast-in-the-mode-of-merrymaking – a wake to allow MT to relax among friends after the ordeal of her enforced resignation three weeks ago.

This came out clearly the moment she walked into our modest – all too modest – and underheated 'reception' room at CPS headquarters in Wilfred Street. This is a former workman's cottage of the kind I once lived in for a few shillings per week in Flask Walk as an impecunious postgraduate student, with tiny rooms and narrow, steep and creaking steps. I've always found the building an embarrassment, especially when receiving foreign visitors, for it is mean, cramped, undignified and without central heating. My friends and colleagues on the board, however, take the view that the house is 'nicely understated' and typically British. So, there we have been, for our sins, since the Centre's foundation in 1974 – 'Hard Times' for us all.

Warming her hands in front of our little gas-fire (she was almost shivering and so were we all), MT immediately launched into expressing her doubts about John Major's administration.

'The new government – well, I think they have embarked on a course of great danger. It is quite clear already that they want to undo many of the things we have accomplished, and there is no telling where that might take them. All the wrong people are rejoicing! That's a sure indication that they are walking down the wrong road,' and more to the same effect.

Signs of great unhappiness in the Thatcher camp could, of course, be detected in the press immediately after MT's resignation.

Perry Worsthorne,[1] for example, let it be known that John Major's 'classless society' and 'caring society', appalled him, but I was astonished to hear MT herself being quite so openly hostile to her chosen successor and so soon after the takeover. Even our own appointees, it would seem, become rivals (for fame, if for nothing else) the moment they succeed us.

She then spoke about the Thatcher Foundation, which she wants to become an ideological centre for Thatcherite ideas worldwide. She said she had already received £10 million from, I believe, the Hanson people but more needed to be raised and more, she thought, could be raised, especially in America. The British example was catching; spreading the word had to be done systematically. Rolling back the frontiers of the state, ending collectivist thinking and punitive taxation were world problems. Britain (i.e. herself) was in the lead, she assured us.

I asked whether the Foundation would have a foreign-policy arm. Very much so, she said, and it would stress its concern with the former communist lands where entirely new national economic structures had to be created. She intended to offer fellowships, sponsor studies both 'in-house' and via other institutions, and establish offices in various Eastern European capitals.

The lunch itself proceeded in a mood of unnatural exuberance. It reminded me of the old Hungarian dictum: 'Don't mention rope in a hanged man's house.' There was general jollity, bonhomie and high-voltage confusion. MT was seated between Hugh Thomas and Raymond Carr. With Carr, she appeared to be on seasoned terms of friendship. Almost inaudibly, private jokes were traded or, to be precise, cracked by Carr, for MT was not shooting back. She never does, bless her soul. She would state the moral, or harangue, but not trump a joke. So my first impression was: here was a display of high spirits to drown the sound of the funeral music in the background.

Second, I felt we were being treated as substitutes for her weekly

---

1. Later Sir Peregrine Worsthorne, conservative writer and journalist, former editor of the *Sunday Telegraph*.

cabinet. She was in prime-ministerial form (schoolmarmish, to be unkind), putting us in order whenever she thought we hadn't reasoned well enough or had fallen down on our homework. Hugh Thomas found himself (once again) at the business-end of his mistress's stick. Is she still hard on him because of his stance on Grenada – or Europe? Probably both.

'What you're arguing isn't at all scholarly,' she would say. 'First, I don't think it's true … Is it true? … Give me three examples … You see, you can't … I knew you couldn't … You're supposed to be an academic and you're telling us things of this kind.'

Hugh took the carping in good part and with great self-restraint. He was the host, it was not for him to be impolite, but I did feel for him. He knows his facts thoroughly, even though at times he does not put them across with the sort of self-assurance MT likes.

Then she had a bit of cruel fun at the expense of (I believe) Taube: 'I can't make out what you're trying to say. There are too many points rolled into one. Now, let's take them one by one … So your first point was … Now what was the second point … and the third? But can you explain what you mean? … Oh, so that's what you wanted to say?' All very unpleasant, though much of it was happily lost in the crossfire.

I felt uncomfortable: if she was like this to her close friends, what was she like with her subordinates, or in cabinet? Perhaps she was like this in cabinet too, which would explain a great deal. I had certainly heard from Ken Clarke[1] (and there is evidence all over Westminster) that polite and not so polite bullying were weapons she seldom resisted using. Ken, of course, can take care of himself – but what about others less well versed in the craft of checkmating the bully?

My impression that MT came to lunch because there wasn't a cabinet to go to is reinforced by the thought that for ten years she did not once cross our threshold, despite her intimate connection with the Centre. We saw her, of course, on many occasions outside

---

1. Former minister of health; later minister of education, home secretary, chancellor of the exchequer.

the building, but to my best knowledge she never came to our premises. Once or twice Powell did, Hurd did, so did Mellor[1] and Waldegrave,[2] but she didn't. Now she suddenly came to confabulate.

Later in the day, at a critical board meeting in a committee room in the Lords (a new chairman is to be elected after Hugh's resignation), Tim Bell[3] told us that MT has indeed taken her fall very badly. She feels deprived, she doesn't know what to do with herself, and she is especially upset by the way in which former supporters have turned on her. Bell gave us examples of the sort of Shakespearean court intrigue rife in the parliamentary party and at all levels further down. 'Have you seen X talking to a Heseltine supporter? Did you see Y from the Thatcher camp having tea with Z? Does that mean he is going to defect?' All this is reported back to the principals; intrigue feeds upon intrigue; the circle of gossip and counter-gossip is self-replenishing. MT's behaviour at lunch was an overreaction, in my judgement, to this state of affairs in the party. She must have felt a deep need to be among people on whose unquestioning approval she could rely. I'm not so sure, though, that she could rely on the unquestioning approval of every member of our lunch party.

The business part of the discussion was short and unstructured, even though Hugh in his admirably polite way tried to impose on it a semblance of order. Lieven and I were asked to offer comments on the state of the USSR. I described some of the things that struck me as important on my recent (October–November) visit to Ukraine. In the cacophony around the table, I rehearsed as best I could my impressions of the first Rukh[4] Congress in Kiev – a milestone in Ukrainian (and Soviet) history. It was, I said, a surprising celebration of a revived sense of Ukrainian national identity openly flaunted in

---

1. David Mellor, minister at the Foreign and Commonwealth Office, 1987–88; Dept. of Health, 1988–89; Home Office, 1989–90.
2. William Waldegrave, minister at the Dept. of the Environment, 1987–88; Dept. of Health, 1988–89; Foreign and Commonwealth Office, 1988–90.
3. Sir Timothy Bell, businessman, public relations adviser.
4. Ukrainian National Movement.

the face of the Soviet state. What surprised me most was a fiery speech by a serving officer of the Red Army in full uniform, Colonel Vilem Martirosian, an ethnic Armenian now in command of a regiment in Rovno and a people's deputy.

He said without beating about the bush, I reported, that should the Ukrainian people, in their drive for independence, come into conflict with Moscow's authority, he would order his troops 'to be on the side of the people'. The task of the army was to protect the nation from outside aggression, not to suppress it. That was how he and many of his brother officers understood their duty. The 2,000-odd delegates stood up, roaring their approval.

Talking to the colonel privately in the lunch-break I asked him whether he was aware that he was advocating and committing mutiny. He said that the name anyone chose to give his thinking left him indifferent. The facts in the USSR were now such that the measures he and his friends in the army were prepared to take would carry the approval of the people and would also be endorsed by several members of the general staff in Moscow and elsewhere. I asked whether he was sure that General Gromov[1] of Afghani fame, and now the commanding general in his region, wouldn't have him arrested for insubordination and worse. He said he had no such fears; things had reached a point that excluded the possibility of victimization. The army was split; tough action could only generate civil war, which no one wanted. I told him that only a few weeks ago, in the liberal United States, General Michael Dugan, chief of staff of the US Air Force, had been dismissed by Dick Cheney, the defence secretary, for having said something infinitely less culpable than what he, Martirosian, was advocating, namely that in case of war the Americans would bomb Baghdad and target Saddam Hussein personally. Didn't he think that under less liberal Soviet conditions he might end up in front of a firing squad? The colonel said he was unworried. The army was disunited, he repeated. No one would be in a position to

---

1. Colonel General Boris Gromov, commander of Soviet forces in the Kiev region, 1989–90; later first deputy minister of interior, USSR; minister of defence, Russian Federation.

'repress' him and his colleagues. They had, he claimed, the population on their side, I reported.

There were gasps of surprise around the table. Margaret Thatcher, however, said she was less surprised than appalled. The breakdown of discipline in the Red Army was a danger for all of us. She was horrified that a serving officer in uniform could air views of this kind in public and apparently get away with it. She said that on her last (June 1990) visit to the USSR she had met Gavriil Popov, head of the Moscow City Council, who had articulated views very similar to those of my Armenian colonel. Popov told her he thought the country could not hold together, that in both the civilian and military domains Russia was teeming with factions, separatists and sectarian expectations.

I'm not at all sure whether MT is looking forward, as I am, to the disintegration of the Soviet empire. Her visit to Ukraine on 9–10 June was a flop. She had been abominably prepared by the Foreign Office. She was unaware of the strength of Ukrainian separatism and was out of sympathy with it. She set a distinction between the case of the Baltic republics for independence, and that of Ukraine. She hurt the feelings and disappointed the expectations of her Ukrainian hosts (as I was repeatedly told by them on my own visit) by declaring in the Ukrainian Parliament that Ukraine's place was *within* the Union and there could be no question of Britain and Ukraine exchanging ambassadors. Britain, she said, did not have an embassy in California or Quebec – she could not see why it should have one in Kiev! Some misjudgement.

On a BBC Russian service phone-in programme, too, about which she had informally consulted me at a No. 10 garden party[1] (we were saying farewell to John O'Sullivan of the Policy Unit), she told some irate Georgians or Armenians (I cannot recall which) that she could not see why the national republics would want to break away from Moscow, seeing how well Texans and Californians were getting along with Washington. We haven't got a British ambassador in Denver,

---

1. Cf. Chapter 6, p. 97.

Colorado, she apparently said, and there is no reason why we should send one to Tbilisi or Yerevan. Some comparison! My advice to MT had been to accept the BBC's invitation, but I did warn her that dry-runs would be useful to forestall surprises. I don't think she took my advice.

MT is undecided whether she does or does not want the complete breakup of the Soviet state. The central theme of her June visit was admiration for the *Soviet Union* in its daunting task of reform. Her investment in Gorbachev is great, and in some ways this is understandable. Gorbachev has undermined the system and destroyed the self-confidence of its élite in a way none of us would have dared to expect even if the CIA and MI5 had put dozens of our agents into key positions in the USSR. In MT's world, Soviet disintegration would destabilize Gorbachev and undermine the world balance of power.

But as the lunch proceeded I had to disappoint MT's trust in the Gorbachev factor. I said my contacts in Russia were unanimous in warning that Gorbachev's days were numbered. Yeltsin was the man of the future. The reformers thought Gorbachev was half-hearted, indecisive and lacking foresight. The old bureaucracy felt he was undermining the legitimacy of their rule. The military complained that he was unable to restrain the national separatists or the reformers' attacks on the army. Only quite recently, I said, Yazov[1] had let it be known on Soviet television that the army's patience was wearing thin, and Kryuchkov,[2] speaking for the KGB, had warned that the Soviet Union was in danger of falling apart – with the corollary that disintegration would not be tolerated.

None of this seemed to please MT. She is for *gradual* reform *under* Gorbachev – certainly for the collapse of the communist

---

1. Marshal Dmitri Yazov, minister of defence, arrested in August 1991 for the attempted 'August coup'; released by amnesty in February 1994.

2. Colonel General Vladimir Kryuchkov, chairman of the KGB, 1988–91, arrested in August 1991 for the attempted 'August coup'; released by amnesty in February 1994. Both amnesties were the work of the dominant 'red–brown' (communist–fascist) faction in the Duma. Yeltsin did not veto the bill.

system, but not, as I say, for the disorderly disintegration of the Soviet empire as a power-factor in the world. I feel, and felt from the beginning of her 'we-can-do-business-with-Gorbachev' phase, that her rather emotional identification with Gorbachev – very much a woman's attitude to politics – went far beyond the call of duty and was putting unnecessary brakes on the pursuit of Western interests. It is, of course, highly unpleasant to drop a friend once he has done his job, but Gorbachev never advocated anything going beyond an enlightened reform of the *communist* system. Dropping him should not have landed MT with a *crise de conscience*. But that would be ignoring the personal chemistry between the two which, I am convinced, played an important part in MT's thinking.

I then stated my view that whether the Soviet system explodes or implodes, or stays formally as it is, the now unpredictable behaviour of almost 300 million people over a vast belt of the Euro-Asian land mass is bound to have an impact on all of us. This argues for the retention of a reconceptualized NATO, a more closely woven European Community, and the speedy establishment of a crisis-management agency under the CSCE. It does *not* argue for the retention, least of all with Western support, of the Soviet empire on the reasoning that it would represent a smaller evil than the chaos that might, but need not, result from its fragmentation. If the Soviet Union retained its integrity, future threats from a post-Gorbachev, nationalistic Russia could not be ruled out, I concluded.

MT was not with me. Her fear of disorder and a more powerful Germany seemed greater than her dedication to human rights and universal liberty.

The second main topic we discussed was the psychological state of Soviet society, with Chai Lieven as our *rapporteur*. Chai is a scintillating young Russian historian at the LSE, a member of our Soviet study group and a British-born scion of the great Baltic princely family of the Lievens. He is a superb if slightly over-forceful speaker and should go far. I knew his polymathic father, Alexander, well when he was controller of the European Services of the BBC and a polished but, for the Soviets, devastating influence on the ether

– one of our Cold War heroes whom the British establishment never honoured or even recognized. If only he had been a pop star or a centre forward! Chai is very much a chip off the old block.

Was collectivism an acquired Soviet characteristic, Chai Lieven asked, or was it deeply rooted in Russian tradition and history? A mixture of the two, he decided, and took us through the familiar ground of Oblomovism[1] in Russian life, various explanations of Russian lethargy and passivity, of the current lack of entrepreneurship and possible remedies, if any. He did, however, point out that while the situation in Russia was difficult, it was not hopeless. For half a century before the Bolshevik takeover, and especially between 1900 and 1914, Russia had made spectacular progress in industry, commerce and agriculture. It had been exporting grain and importing technology and capital. The entrepreneurial spirit, he said, was now dormant but not dead.

Lieven was excellent in showing the 'otherness' of Russian culture and of the Russian work ethic. I felt MT was left wondering whether, in post-Soviet Russia, the spirit of enterprise of the five pre-Soviet decades, or the dead weight of collectivism would prevail. If the latter, privatization, the creation of wealth and other features of a free-market economy on Thatcherite lines would be facing a bleak future.

I butted in to say that what we are seeing in the Soviet Union and Eastern/Central Europe is the collapse of civil society. 'Civil society!?' The words jarred on her ears. 'What on earth is "civil society"?' she demanded to know. I should have remembered her mocking opposition to the very notion of 'society' – which she always maintained did not exist; for her only individuals and families existed, not 'society' – but I didn't. Here I was, adding insult to injury by talking about the doubly hateful notion of 'civil society'. The idea and the words are, of course, common currency in scholarship, and I incautiously assumed that after the large number of books

---

1. After I. A. Goncharov's *Oblomov*, symbol of the good-natured indolence and ineffectiveness of the Russian élite under Nicholas I.

she had read on Soviet matters she would know what I was talking about. But she didn't, or said she didn't, wanting perhaps to draw me out.

'Do you mean Establishment?' she went on. 'No,' I said, 'I don't mean Establishment; I mean all those customs and assumptions among individuals which are not regulated by law but upon which civilized living depends. They are distinct from the state; they are spontaneous.'

'Can you give me an example?' she demanded.

'Well, for example, in this country it is assumed that people including civil servants will answer letters; that the tax inspector will return your overpayment; that your local policeman will help you across the street if you're with children; that you can get your son into the school of your choice without greasing the palms of the headmaster; that charities exist and attract donations which will not be pocketed by the organizers; that voluntary associations are really voluntary and mean to do some good, and so on. None of these things can be taken for granted in the USSR.'

'Well then, why didn't you say so?' said MT, somewhat mollified. She probably had a point.

Lieven then outlined the difficulty Western people, including scholars, have in thinking away from Western stereotypes and making the intellectual leap to Sovietism. This is one of our greatest handicaps, he said, in trying to design effective policies. The mark of a good general is his ability to incorporate in his planning an imaginative understanding of what he would be doing if he were in charge of the enemy command. The same, he said, is true of our relations with the Soviets. We must make an effort to comprehend the consequences of the breakdown of ordinary life in Russia, of the cluelessness, unpreparedness and often superstitious fears of the Soviet population.

I chipped in to say that the USSR has now entered a stage of rapid disintegration, but MT felt I was understating the case. 'No, no, the Soviet Union *has disintegrated*. It's gone,' she exclaimed without any visible sign of pleasure. And indeed, before lunch was over, we heard that Shevardnadze had resigned under dramatic circumstances.

Chai's mention of superstition prompted me to add that both Russia and Ukraine were, understandably enough, steeped in an atmosphere of utter gloom. The population was embracing an 'eschatology of woe' – a premonition, not unlike the one that followed the eighteenth-century Lisbon earthquake, that the world was ripe for punishment. The Slavic nations were once again called upon to bear most of it. Chernobyl and the poisoning of the earth by pesticides and industrial pollution added to the fear of the apocalypse. Faith-healers, hypnotists and miracle-workers proliferated, some acquiring national fame and following through television. It was, I said, difficult to see how a people so easily given to relapses of this kind could be modernized and made democratic in our sense of the word in the short or even the long term.

As we were about to break up, Raymond Carr, putting his arm around Margaret Thatcher, said words to the effect that: 'one conclusion I would draw from what you have told me today is that you deplore, with Martin Wiener, the nineteenth-century gentrification of English society and are very conscious of its baleful influence on British competitiveness and power in our own century.' To which MT simply answered: 'You're absolutely right.' Here was one nice piece of evidence of Margaret Thatcher's radical brand of Toryism.

On leaving the room I mentioned to MT that about a month ago I had written a paper for her as prime minister, covering some of the things (and much else) I was saying over lunch. I had given it, on 14 December, to Sir Percy Cradock, who had probably passed it on to John Major, not to her. She said she had not seen it; could I let her have it now? I'm going to send it along.

What I still find admirable in MT is her willingness – indeed her compulsive desire – to be among intellectually sharp people, whether of agreeable or contrary opinions, in bad times as well as good ones. I don't think Baldwin, or Macmillan, or Wilson, or Callaghan, or Douglas-Home or even Heath held seminars to broaden their minds and take advice from unorthodox quarters. They were too grand or too complacent and frequently both. Nor does it seem likely that those intellectual duds Americans keep elevating to the presidency – Eisenhower, Johnson, Ford, Reagan – have done so, though Roosevelt and Kennedy did. Margaret Thatcher's need of admiration is now great, but her stomach for controversy and a good fight is even stronger – a rare trait in a politician.

CHAPTER 11

Fit for a Queen

At home, 1991 was not a good year for Margaret Thatcher. In the parliamentary wing of the Conservative Party and on the hustings, there was general relief that an abrasive leader – and by most forecasts an election loser – had been replaced by John Major, the 'one-nation' Tory of relaxed manners and non-controversial European credentials.

As her support was ebbing away and her role in history was being questioned, she began to feel increasingly more comfortable in the republican surroundings of the United States, where she had become an object of idolization and flattery, rather than in the country she had once led.

Diary

Washington, 23 September 1991

Margaret Thatcher had her great royal homecoming tonight – in America. She advanced as close to an apotheosis as a mortal can in the Regency Ballrooms of the Omni Shoreham Hotel in downtown Washington. I've seen nothing like it since the Indiana University Hoosiers played the USC football team in Bloomington, Indiana in 1975, with myself as an incredulous spectator.

The venue was the Heritage Foundation's 'Clare Boothe Luce Award Dinner', at which MT was the guest of honour and the main speaker, though not the awardee. It was a black-tie occasion. Everybody who is anybody in Washington and beyond was there – some fourteen hundred of them. I counted three bands, one being the celebrated United States Navy Band in their white full-dress uniform. A splendid colour-party represented the American armed forces. The Queen couldn't have done better, what with the country-club conservatives, corporate America and the military all gathered under one roof. The honours were done by Ed Feulner[1] and Frank Shakespeare,[2] president and former president of the Foundation – both friends of mine and long-standing political allies.

This was, in effect, a transatlantic version of trooping the colour – a 'private' display of the raw majesty of American power. After Ed's eulogy there was a 'Presentation of the Colors by the Armed Forces' Color team', with MT sitting at the centre of the dais flanked by dignitaries. As the flags were dipped before her, the national anthem was played; we all stood. Then came the Heritage Foundation's own march and, finally, as an overture to MT's speech, the 'Thatcher Freedom March', specially composed and personally conducted by the 'Honorable J. William Middendorf, II', an old trustee of the Foundation and a pleasant enough man whom I had met in Switzerland.

I was stunned – not by what MT said in her speech, for she launched just another tirade against the concept of a united states of Europe, coupling it with an initiative (stillborn, in my view) for an Atlantic economic community, all of which seemed to make no impression on the Americans at my table, though I knew it would be greeted with delight by Europhobes in London and embarrass Major's government (it was only last Sunday that Norman Lamont[3] said the government would sign up for a common currency provided eight of the twelve EC states were willing to take part). I was stunned, rather, by the realization that America was conferring on MT the sort of honorary imperial presidency she had vainly sought at home.

The glory was hers, even though the power was borrowed. Inward-looking Britain in her shrunken state, one among several in

---

1. Edwin J. Feulner Jr, president of the Heritage Foundation; US presidential adviser.

2. Former United States ambassador; former director of the US Information Agency; former chairman of the Board for International Broadcasting.

3. British chancellor of the exchequer, 1990–93.

a squabbling and for her psychologically alien Europe, is small beer for her. But here in Washington, seat of the only remaining super-power, with the symbols, and the reality, of the might of America so theatrically displayed, she could, for a brief hour or two, savour the rewards of history she felt were her due. She was praised by her hosts to the point of embarrassment. When the black ties stood up to toast her, it was like a regimental gathering drinking to the monarch. And so, for her, it was – America, after all, was a British creation. The betrayal at home could be forgotten.

This was a scene out of Hollywood, certainly flamboyant and overdone to European eyes, but a wonderful opportunity for the historian to see MT the way she would probably like to be re-membered. Friedrich Gundolf,[1] a hero of my youth, had a great piece of truth on his side when he said that more important than the deeds of Caesar were the myths to which they had given rise, and he went on writing a famous book about Caesar's 'Ruhm' – the legends he had created in the minds of men in various cultures.

I abhor celebrations of this kind (though I admire them in Wagner and Verdi), particularly when harnessed to PR and fundraising. But what a revealing view (if I've got it right) of the psyche of a woman whose mind I so often tried to read and, in some small ways, to influence!

---

1. German literary historian, 1880–1931; member of the Stefan George circle of symbolist poets and critics.

CHAPTER 12

In Exile

Margaret Thatcher's attitude to the wars on the territory of former Yugoslavia was unswervingly consistent from their beginning, in 1991. Unlike the American administration and initially the European Community, she did nothing to encourage the communist power-wielders in Belgrade to hold together what was obviously falling apart. She pointed at Serbia as the aggressor, first against newly independent Slovenia and Croatia – both recognized after democratic elections by the international community – and then against the Bosnian state through the self-appointed Serbian rebel government in Pale, on Bosnian soil.

She was equally clear that 'ethnic cleansing' by the Serbian army and various Serb-sponsored paramilitary commandos was racist persecution on a genocidal scale which Western governments had a statutory, as well as a profoundly moral, duty to stop and to defeat. Her condemnation of the United Nations arms embargo, which was denying Bosnia the means of self-defence, was unambiguous. She urged practical support for the victims of aggression on the principles on which the Second World War had been fought, and accused Western governments, not least the British government under John Major and Douglas Hurd, of complicity with aggression.

Such courage and clarity of understanding were rare in the Western world, and, although they were coming from a politician unburdened by the responsibilities of office, they were heard as a serious warning against appeasement way beyond the shores of Britain.

It was on a Bosnian errand that I saw Lady Thatcher next, after a gap of more than two years. But her mood was being shaped by things closer than Bosnia. In April 1992 the Conservative Party had registered yet another election victory – but this time under the leadership of John Major. The Thatcher factor was proving distinctly dispensable. This was not what she had been hoping for.

Diary

8 April 1993

Had a longish meeting this morning with MT – now Baroness Thatcher – at her new HQ in Chesham Place. Her title doesn't sit well with the populist image she has been cultivating of herself, though I find it less absurd than the peerages conferred on the 'socialist' lords Wilson, Callaghan and Healy. This front-loading of names in a supposedly modern country is a symbol of much that is wrong with Britain.

A few weeks ago I helped to launch a small international committee[1] to try to mount a private war crimes' investigation of the Serbian killers in the Bosnian war. We need support and funds. I feel MT might give us the first (she's been eloquent on Serbian guilt and Western betrayal) and perhaps some of the second. Distinguished people in several countries are ready to cooperate. We hope exposure may stay the hands of some of the Balkan thugs and prepare the ground for any UN investigation or a formal war crimes trial. Last week I wrote to Margaret Thatcher inviting her to join our committee and asking whether she would support us with advice and funds. This morning's session was the result of that letter.

Despite my deep interest in the Bosnian crisis, however, Bosnia will not be given pride of place in this account. I found to my surprise MT's state of mind more fascinating, if less important, than anything we said or could have said about the well-flogged topic of the Balkan war.

I have not seen her for more than two years – probably because she had no reason to want to see me, and I wasn't looking for a meeting either. I should imagine she suspected that I was opposed to her various articulations about Europe. So I was. I found them driven by prejudice and damaging for Britain. Also, I felt the Major government was doing fairly well.

Yugoslavia's disintegration, however, has put me on her side

---

1. International Committee for Human Rights and Obligations.

again. She has spoken magnificently, and from a position of great moral strength, about the West's, and especially the British government's, cowardly attitude to Serbian aggression, and has shamed our leaders. I now feel I can call on her again as an ally on limited territory.

Her offices in Chesham Place immediately struck me as something designed to impress the visitor as an alternative seat of government. What I saw of the actual 'business' area was not large – four or five rooms for her assistants and secretaries – but the building itself gave me the impression that I was in one of those elegant Viennese town-palaces that the Pálfys, Zichys and Lobkowiczes used during the 'season' in Habsburg days, and from which favours were dispensed and withdrawn. It is an Edwardian house in Belgravia, with a fine staircase reminiscent of the one in 10 Downing Street and spacious reception rooms. There is a police guard outside and a commission-aire or two to show one up – an environment to impress visitors, especially foreign visitors, as the headquarters of a former prime minister who happens to be out of office but not out of power, and expects to be called back when the time is right.

Upstairs I was met by Robin Harris, MT's present chief of staff and an accomplished writer, and Mark Worthington, a younger man with whom I had a stimulating talk about a year ago at Ralph (Lord) Harris's[1] dinner table. Both are men of complete dedication and impressive efficiency. Robin shares my strong feelings about our betrayal of the Bosnians and, earlier, of the Croats. He has strong Christian convictions, which express themselves in punishingly hard work. Jeffrey Archer[2] was coming out of her room and soon the lady appeared and we exchanged compliments. She said I was sun-tanned and looking younger. I returned the compliment with interest. She did look well and fully charged. 'Oh, well,' she said, brushing my words aside, 'we haven't seen each other for quite some time, so what you are saying is very pleasing.' She didn't say why there had

---

1. Lord Harris of High Cross, founder of the Institute of Economic Affairs.
2. Lord Archer of Weston-super-Mare, politician and author.

been so large a gap and I didn't comment, but I think the reason was well understood.

Her great reception room, too, was reminiscent of No. 10 – prime ministerial, indeed, presidential. It was, I felt, entirely in line with her famous past, though perhaps less so with what I thought would be her political future. I said I found her new HQ spacious and beautifully appointed. This put MT slightly on the defensive. 'You know, this was not an expensive building. It's been good value and all the furniture and furnishings have been chosen by myself. It may be a little too large for our purposes at the moment, but eventually the Thatcher Foundation will be housed here as well, and that will need offices.'

I came away with the general impression that Margaret Thatcher has not accepted – has not been able psychologically to digest – the fact that she is no longer prime minister. Her whole attitude to the day's business – the rush into which she appeared to have driven herself throughout the morning, her remarks about various small and large things she had to attend to immediately, with the underlying thought that unless these things were performed quickly and efficiently something terrible might befall the world and certainly Britain – all point to the sad fact that two and a half years after her resignation she still cannot reconcile herself to the loss of that terrible elixir – power.

Another indication that points in the same direction is the manner in which she talked about her activities, always using the plural. 'We have a great deal to do tomorrow,' she would say, 'our days are over-subscribed, aren't they Robin, with a hundred items on our agenda. Look at this pile of documents we have assembled about the nationality problems in the former Soviet Union. We have read all that and now we have to decide things very quickly. Time is pressing because who knows how Yeltsin will be doing at the referendum on the 25th. We are taking advice from various sources; we've had people here from the Russian Institute in Sandhurst, and we have not yet decided how to deal with the issue.' All this in *pluralis majestatis* – we, we, we. Margaret Thatcher cannot adjust because she is no ordinary politician; she is, at heart, an ideologue with a message. Her time in office may have come to an end, but not her mission.

I was distressed. Was this great lady entertaining false ideas about her place in the universe? Was she lapsing into a phantom world, waiting for the bugle to sound summoning her back to the field of action? This sounds unkind, but who knows? Chesham Place certainly appears to be MT's Colombey-les-Deux Eglises, but I rather doubt whether the call to rescue England from the embrace of John Major will ever come, and if such a call did come her way, I'm fairly certain she would lose the next election.

I found her hyperactivity exasperating. After a few more low-key sentences, she would erupt again: 'We can't waste time on that, Mark, can we? We have an appointment. We are making a speech tomorrow we haven't finished drafting yet. What is the Supreme Court saying in Karlsruhe? Let's look at the Ceefax.'

How did this tormented search for 'work' and to be wanted come out of the self-confident Margaret Thatcher I knew ten years ago? It saddens me to see a person of great intelligence and iron determination, a person filled with a sense of mission, and respected, yes, still respected – even admired, especially in America – not being able to assimilate the fact that her great strengths are no longer employable in the way in which they were only a few years ago; and that most of the scaffolding around her – her office, her personal power, that semi-royal status she carved out for herself in her own and the world's imagination, the courtiers and flatterers – have all fallen away like leaves from a tree struck by a mysterious disease. Margaret Thatcher is persuaded that she has been the victim of a betrayal comparable only to the assassination of an absolute monarch by his most trusted lieutenants.

I felt she was happy enough to see me, but I also felt after our first half-hour or so that my presence was mainly an opportunity for her to give free rein to her emotions and test her restless intelligence. Her frustrations needed airing, and I was both close enough and distant enough to absorb them. I am no public figure – at best a witness and a chronicler. Confiding in me could do no great damage.

I keep asking myself: now that the common Soviet enemy is gone, and on Europe we are at opposite ends of the spectrum, why is it that I still feel close to MT, and why is it (stranger still) that she seems to treat me as an ally? Our conversation today must have struck Robin Harris and Mark Worthington (both were sitting in) as a sharp but good-natured brainstorming session between friends, MT of course doing most of the talking, but not being upset when she saw my face expressing disbelief or heard me uttering opinions that were out of tune with hers.

I think the key to my closeness to her is best described as an affinity of temperament. I am wholly in sympathy with her intolerance of fools, of the slow execution of orders, of the piecemeal approach to things that require overarching strategies. I sympathize with her scorn for the morally timid and the diplomatic prevaricators. I too have been accused at various times in my life of revving at speeds hostile to my human environment, of being a hard taskmaster, bad at delegating responsibility and ignoring protocol to the chagrin of the bureaucracy.

MT has an *admirable* record of intolerance to her name. That was the secret of her many successes, and that of course proved to be the cause of her fall, too. But in 1979, lazy old England, with its half-hearted ways, horrible economic record and inability to embrace any long-term vision, needed her intolerance. Attila the Hun was said to be the scourge of God – when MT came to power, I was hoping against hope that she would whip Britain into shape. She did what she could, but her time was short and her *hubris*, alas, great.

Another strain I like in MT's character is her inclination to speak her mind with extreme frankness when she is among friends and the context is right. This morning's session was definitely such an occasion. It was wild. She was using words, making gestures and going at a speed that betrayed a fire burning inside her which she could not, or did not see the need to, control. Some of the establishment would have been horrified, but for me she was speaking on a frequency that made perfect sense.

I'm returning here to something I said in an earlier entry: the contradiction between Margaret Thatcher's proud Englishness and the very un-English ways in which she is trying to give it effect. If Englishness means common sense, moderation, give-and-take, respect for minority views, the distrust of grand schemes and theories, then MT represents the opposite of these: passionate attachments, perfectionism and unbending leadership. This inner contradiction makes her an intriguing figure as well as one of perplexing charm. A man would not be getting away with it; a woman does. I believe she understands and condones the smile on my face when I see her wrestling with her dilemma.

On the question of Bosnia, MT was very much in sympathy. I explained what we were about and she gave our committee an enthusiastic letter of support. It should be helpful in fundraising. She was first wondering whether a simulated trial might not prejudice the real one, if such ever came to be mounted by the UN; but when I explained that ours would be more in the nature of a public investigation than a trial, and that we had already secured the co-operation of distinguished people such as Max Kampelman[1] and Richard Perle in the US, she withdrew her reservations and also promised to provide funds through her foundation. I said our aim was to bring the victims of torture and rape as well as witnesses to killings and deportations before the cameras and that two of our leading members (George Stamkoski and Ben Cohen) were already working on this. This made an impression. She suggested I should approach Lord Shawcross[2] for advice and participation. I've already done so. He sounded cooperative.

I hope MT will be generous in providing funds. So far her foundation has acquired a reputation for being rather tight-fisted, despite the large amounts at her disposal. I was told in America that

---

1. American ambassador to the Helsinki round of negotiations, 1980–83; to nuclear and disarmament negotiations, 1985–89.

2. Formerly (Sir) Hartley Shawcross, British prosecutor at the Nuremberg War Crimes Tribunal.

the Heritage Foundation alone had helped her to secure a great deal of money on her lecture tours; yet no one has so far been able to identify more than a couple of recipients. Whether this is still true, I don't know. But compared to George Soros's[1] activities, the Thatcher Foundation is hardly visible.

Talking of fundraising for our project, MT suggested that we should go to Conrad Black[2] (which I had already done via his wife, Barbara Amiel, but so far without success), and Rupert Murdoch[3] with whom I have never been in contact and do not intend to be now.[4] She thought George Soros would be my best bet, whereupon I told her that I knew Soros and briefly related how impressively he had spoken at a session Brian Griffiths and I had arranged for him with Douglas Hurd, the foreign secretary, a few weeks ago. MT wanted to know the details. 'Soros had just come back from Sarajevo,' I said, 'and was appalled by the Western powers' inactivity. He faxed me to ask whether I could help him to see someone in the UK government, preferably the PM or Douglas Hurd. Brian and I arranged a meeting with the foreign secretary.

'Hurd seemed to be interested in the character of the great donor-speculator. What made him tick? He wanted to know why Soros was giving large sums of money (much in excess of what most governments were donating) for Bosnian relief. What made him install a water purification plant in Sarajevo, rebuild schools and provide a whole range of expensive public services? "You see, Foreign Secretary," Soros said, "I'm a Hungarian Jew. I want the Muslim world to know that Jews have it in them to give massive help when human rights are violated, no matter who the victims may be. I would find it intolerable to watch the Serbian thugs doing things we all said at

1. Hungarian-born American financier and philanthropist.

2. Historian, chairman of the *Daily Telegraph*.

3. Publisher; chairman of *News Corporation*, owner of *The Times*, the *Sun*, the *News of the World*, Sky Television and other media.

4. The committee ended up receiving one medium-sized grant from the American 'Smith Richardson Foundation' and a small one from Margaret Thatcher. George Soros and Conrad Black declined to help. The committee had to wind up its work barely a year after its foundation.

the end of the War would never again be tolerated – and do nothing about them."

'Hurd was taking notes. I felt he was greatly impressed – or ought to have been. Here was the kind of statesmanlike articulation *he* ought to have been making, not the New York financier. But he stuck to the low ground, producing his well-rehearsed catalogue of prevarications – that nothing warlike *should* be done; that nothing *could* be done; that what could be done would find no support in the Commons; and if it did find support there, Britain didn't have the forces, or the funds to do it – a sorry list of feeble evasions! Appeasement all over again,' I said.

MT shared my ire. Hurd's lack of any resolve sticks in her throat every bit as much as it does in mine. Hurd, we agreed, had misread the Yugoslav crisis from the beginning. It was a case of aggression, not civil war, and from that misreading followed all the blunders we and all the other European governments have been making.

MT picked up Soros's Jewish point with alacrity. She went into a long speech praising her Jewish friends and political allies. The Jews, she said, are marvellous: they give selflessly, they support good causes, they are thrifty and generous in every conceivable way. 'Why don't you approach Lord Jakobovits, the former Chief Rabbi, and draw him into your committee?' I said I might do that, though I have no contacts with the UK Jewish community. But MT has a point: having a celebrated senior Jew on the committee would make our work truly ecumenical and mobilize funds.

I then tried to persuade MT that there was also political mileage to be had from a strong stance on Bosnia. The British public, I said, but also the American, German and French public, are by now so upset by their daily exposure to the savageries of the Serbs that their gut reactions are far ahead of the crab-like progress of government thinking. We should make the most of this. Hurd insists that foreign policy shall not be made by television. We can agree with that, but foreign policy can and must be made on the basis of moral considerations, or else Western democracy is a sham and the Second World War was about nothing at all.

I knew this would strike home with MT because she had repeatedly stated that Western behaviour in Bosnia had to be judged in the light of the commitment the Allies had made in the Second World War never again to permit genocidal ideologies to rule the world. Yet we were allowing just that. Worse, by being party to an arms embargo that treats the victim on a par with the aggressor, we had become accomplices to aggression.

I went on to say that underneath a deceptive show of British indifference, the heart of the nation was responsive and sound. There was a good deal of untapped moral and emotional capital MT could convert into political action if she made a series of appeals using the right language. She should, I suggested, link Bosnia to the British sense of honour, liberty and international responsibility and say that Karadžić[1] and his killers were no more acceptable to us than were Hitler and Stalin. She should hammer away on the theme that Bosnia was not a far away country; that the Serbian aggressors represented a loathsome combination of communism and fascism; that it was not true that thirty German divisions could not sort out Yugoslavia during the war; and finally that, if the Bosnian model were allowed to go unchecked, violent nationalism, racial intolerance and the change of borders by armed force would spread way beyond former Yugoslavia, especially eastwards. I hinted that she could capture the moral high ground on Bosnia and re-establish herself as a key figure on the international scene.

MT was nodding approvingly but did not say whether she would consider doing the things I suggested. I was, as I say, only reinforcing her own thoughts about Bosnia, but I know from experience that even that can be a great help in an ambivalent environment.

Europe's impotence over Bosnia, and the weasel words used by our governments to hoodwink the public and evade responsibility, have had a profound personal effect on me. I am especially galled by the selective character of the liberal conscience. Some years ago, Vietnam, apartheid, Mandela and nuclear weapons touched off the

---

1. Radovan Karadžić, president of self-styled Bosnian Serb Republic in Pale, Bosnia.

anger of large sections of our young. Protesters jammed the streets of every Western capital. But now – all is quiet! I cannot recall a single major demonstration in front of a 'Yugoslav' embassy. All the more reason for MT to go on the offensive – but whether she is the right person to do so is another matter. It may well be that her image among the young has been so blackened that she would achieve the opposite of what she'd be setting out to achieve. In America, however, I'm fairly certain her call to arms would still strike home.

MT asked how I saw developments in Russia. I gave her a bird's eye view of the unholy alliance between the far Left and far Right. Their stated purpose was to topple Yeltsin and the reformers. Rutskoi[1] and Khasbulatov[2] were on the warpath. I said I thought Yeltsin would probably win the referendum on 25 April with a fair majority, but of course one couldn't be sure. Even if he won with a *large* majority, he would still encounter resistance in the bureaucracy and the armed forces. The system may have fallen apart, but there has been no de-Sovietization.

I drew MT's attention to the proclamations and activities of the Army Officers' Union, with their mutinous defiance of the new order, and to signs of spreading war-lordism in the army and the collapse of central discipline. Several commanding generals, especially in Moldova and the Baltic area, were going their own way, and I related how some Western commercial flights had recently been forced to land at airfields between Ukraine and the Russian far east, with each war-lord exacting his hard-currency ransom before allowing the planes to proceed. None recognized Moscow's authority over his air-space. All this, I said, was extremely dangerous and had the makings of civil war. The reliability of this or that military unit in a political crisis was the talk of Moscow.

---

1. Major-General Alexander Rutskoi, vice-president of Russia, later 'acting president' appointed by Parliament; arrested for leading coup of October 1993, granted amnesty in February 1994.

2. Ruslan Khasbulatov, former chairman of Russian Parliament; arrested for attempted coup in October 1993, granted amnesty in February 1994.

MT said her information was very much in line with mine. She was worried and asked me to have some of the materials from which I had quoted from memory sent to her. This I will do.

She then reminisced for a while about her friendship with Gorbachev and Raisa. They had been planning to meet again, she said, but events kept interfering, the latest being Raisa's arm, damaged by a stroke in the Crimea at the time of the August (1991) coup.

'You know, I'm not at all surprised that she had a stroke,' MT observed. 'There they were, prisoners of the conspirators, isolated from the world, surrounded by troops, expecting the worst. Gorbachev, Raisa, their children and grandchildren must have felt that at any moment they could be put up against the wall and shot. The sheer terror of that expectation must have given Raisa her stroke.' MT's very spirited identification surprised me. Did she think that, symbolically speaking, the 'same' sort of thing could have happened to her – *did* happen to her?

She then asked what I thought about rumours she had heard that Gorbachev may have been party to the August coup – plotting, as it were, against himself. She could not, she said, quite believe it. Gorbachev was too straightforward for that. Such things did not happen in real life, although plotting had a long and spectacular history in the Russian tradition.

I said I was myself very sceptical. In *The August Coup*[1] Gorbachev had denied having played any part whatever, but he did say that for almost a year he had foreseen and feared that a coup by 'reactionary forces' might be attempted. My own conjecture was that in his exasperation at the rapid disintegration of the Soviet Union, and especially his horror at the chaotic events in the Baltic states, he might have expressed the opinion to his close collaborators – including, of course, Yazov, Kryuchkov and Yanayev[2] – that at some point Moscow would have to put an end to the mayhem and make

---

1. London, 1991.

2. Gennadii Yanayev, 'president' of USSR during the attempted coup in August 1991; arrested in August 1991, granted amnesty in February 1994.

the country fit for orderly reforms. The plotters, I went on, may have interpreted this as a tacit signal for tough action in the hope that once the *putsch* had been successful, Gorbachev would give it his blessing and take it under his wing. This is, of course, pure speculation, I added, but I wouldn't be surprised if a scenario of this kind came to light at the trial of the plotters. It would certainly be very much in their interest to play their cards with that end in mind.

I will add here for the record that two and a half years ago a coup by Gorbachev did not strike me as entirely unthinkable. I did not say so this morning, and MT did not bring it up, although I had informed her at the time. Probably she had forgotten.

In December 1990, soon after my return from a visit to Russia and Ukraine, I sent the prime minister, through Sir Percy Cradock, an evaluation of what I had seen. By that time (14 December) John Major was prime minister, but I also sent a copy to Margaret Thatcher. This is what I wrote:

> My own, highly tentative forecast is that, if there is to be a coup in the USSR, it will probably be by Gorbachev himself. When all other methods have failed him, he might put himself at the head of the most radical wing of his supporters and declare for an entirely free market economy, a multi-party system and a rapid and permissive transformation of the Union – still in the name of an enlightened socialism, but using the Army and the KGB as his tools. With his newly acquired powers as president, Gorbachev certainly has the means to mount a coup-from-above. Whether he could enlist the support of Yeltsin, the Russian parliament and the Ukraine is another matter.

MT said she could not begin to understand why the conspirators had been released while still under investigation. 'Here they are,' she said, 'on our television screens, leading anti-Yeltsin demonstrations in the streets of Moscow, with the charge of high treason and possibly the death sentence hanging over their heads. They have a nerve! Why are they allowed to do so?'

I shared her anger. It was indeed monstrous – a sign of Yeltsin's great weakness and probably a portent of worse to come. MT said she had met Yazov and formed a highly unflattering opinion of him. I assured her she was in good company. A brute of a man, she said, his character written all over his face. What did I think of Gorbachev's possible complicity in a *larger* context? Were we being tricked into something?

Let me, I said, rehearse to you what I think is a bizarre theory; but, of course, you may not find it so. There is a minority view among scholars, I said, which holds that the Gorbachev era, then Yeltsin's arrival at the helm, then the disintegration of the system and empire, are but a huge exercise in disinformation carefully designed by the KGB to fool the West and secure the long-term survival of Russian power. Its chief protagonists are two highly respected Soviet-Russian historians – Alain Besançon of l'Ecole des hautes études and a former student of his, Françoise Thom, now a professor in her own right at the Sorbonne.

These scholarly and charming people (I know Besançon well and Thom slightly) boxed themselves into an ideological corner in the Gorbachev era, refusing to believe – and it *was* difficult to believe – that the Soviet system could produce genuine reformers, much less reforms of a kind that could get so out of hand as to destroy the system. And when the system and empire did collapse, they were for a time unable to extricate themselves from their *idée fixe* and went on telling us that, hidden from our view, the KGB was still pulling the strings in Russia, Ukraine, the Baltic states and even Central Europe. Different 'echelons', they said, were at work. The KGB, on this showing, is perfectly willing to sacrifice a Communist A-team for the sake of a social democratic B-team; a B-team for a free-market-capitalist C-team; and that for a fascist-nationalist D-team, so long as it has them all under its ultimate control. The KGB's objective is to rebuild Russian power with Western funds and technology, lull us into a false sense of security, and work for the day a reborn Russia will be able to achieve what old-fashioned communism couldn't.

'Rubbish, rubbish,' MT exclaimed. 'You don't give up power in the faint hope of regaining power in the distant future! I don't believe a word of it.'

I assured her that the theory had very few takers; nevertheless, some people close to her and my way of thinking gave it credence, which tends to distort our understanding of what precisely is happening in the ex-Soviet world and what we may expect in the future. I didn't mention names, for the list would have been embarrassing.

Of course, I said, I was perfectly willing to accept that in 1989–90 the KGB, the East German Stasi, the Romanian Securitate and the other secret services were trying to keep the lid on the ferment, and when that didn't work, they tried to insinuate their own men under one cover or another into positions of power. I am also willing to accept, in fact I know, that the networks still exist and, of course, there is self-interest and corruption. But the hidden-hand theory as a master-guide to our understanding is untenable. If the KGB was so clever, why did it not prevent the self-destruction of the Soviet empire in the first place? MT agreed. She repeated that the theory struck her as utterly flawed.

Talking about the Russian army set MT off about our own. She was, she said, appalled by John Major's decision to cut back our three services. 'There is no telling what the Russians might do next,' she said; 'they might turn against us; they might try to recapture some of their former satellites in Eastern Europe; there might be a showdown between rival factions, Parliament and the president – who knows? This is no time to cut our forces, no time at all.' I agreed. She was showing real concern.

We then turned to domestic matters, notably the state of affairs in the Conservative Party. 'Do you know, George, what's the real problem with the Conservative Party? The name of it. "Conservative" is no longer right. It doesn't describe what we are. It's directly misleading. We are not a "conservative" party; we are a party of innovation, of imagination, of liberty, of striking out in new directions, of renewed national pride and a novel sense of leadership. That's not "conservative", is it?! We've taken on not only the unions, but also the doctors and the legal profession because the public was not being properly served by them. That's not "conservative"! The name is all wrong.'

I thoroughly agreed with that, remembering, however, that only a few years ago 'conservative' was a name she had proudly embraced. My own support of 'MT-the-domestic-politician' was always predicated on her radical interpretation of 'conservatism'. And 'Thatcherism', in its first years, was indeed radical, innovative and sometimes hard on the unprepared – as it had to be to shake Britain out of its stagnation. MT's assault on the entrenched vested interests of barristers and solicitors especially warmed my heart.

But I also recalled that in the mid and late 1980s the same MT was upset because, in the Soviet vocabulary, not least in Gorbachev's, 'conservative' was correctly (as I thought) used to identify the old unrepentant Stalinists. It was a way of hanging a shield on stick-in-the-mud communist bureaucrats, stone-bottomed managers and dutifully unimaginative army leaders. MT, as I say, was at the time deeply offended and told me so on a couple of occasions. 'This is all wrong,' she would say, '*we* are the Conservatives. We are a great party; how does anyone in the USSR dare to suggest that these crusty old Stalinists are a "conservative" force?'

Clearly, she has changed her semantics, and I should imagine the change came in the light of some of her experiences abroad. In French, German or Italian ears 'conservative' has a ring of datedness, immobilism and stagnation. I wouldn't be surprised if one of her Christian Democratic or Gaullist admirers had said to her after a lecture: 'Lady Thatcher, what you are saying is just wonderful, but why on earth do you call yourself a conservative? That word has negative associations for us, meaning "left-behind", "fuddy-duddy", "sticking to worn-out traditions". You're really one of us, a *radical*, aren't you?' I wonder whether her words this morning weren't the result of that sort of reaction.

She then voiced her great concern that Britain under John Major was losing its way in the world and would no longer count. And she put down some of that loss of direction to Britain's involvement with the European Community and Major's 'ambiguous' policies. I knew and had feared from the beginning of today's session that sooner or later the sore topic of Europe would come up for discussion. However amicably we would be talking about Bosnia, swords would be crossed on Europe. I am, alas, only too well aware of her position, and she is of mine.

So here she was, haranguing me about Europe again. Fortunately, however, the harangue came at the very end of our long discussion, literally as I was leaving her study. I had decided on my way up to London not to allow what promised to be a helpful meeting to be spoilt by a Euro-wrangle. It was, after all, I who had asked for a meeting and she would probably be very cooperative on Bosnia. But would she, I wondered, have the good sense of leaving Europe alone?

For ninety minutes we managed not to mention Europe, but, as I was already half-way through the door, MT grabbed me: 'Well, you realize, George, don't you, that it is the European involvement that is, above all other things, dragging Britain down. It is our participation in that unholy mess. Let no one forget that.'

I was in a quandary. Should I, with one foot in the lobby, now go into an elaborate defence of the rationale of British membership? I decided this was neither the time nor the place. But I could not let MT's words go entirely unchallenged.

'One useful way of making relations better between Britain and the Community would be to do the sort of thing about Bosnia I have just tried to suggest. There is a strong sense throughout the Continent that in Bosnia the European Community has failed its first real test. If you called for determined action, not as an insular critic, but on behalf of the Community of which Britain feels itself to be an inalienable part, then I'd be very much surprised if feelings on both sides of the Channel didn't improve rapidly. You would be lifting the status of Britain and doing a great thing for what is morally right and for Bosnia. Alternatively, you could just go on pressing John Major's government for more resolve, putting Britain ahead of other nations in the fight for human rights and liberty. That, too, would have a most useful European dimension.'

Whether she thought this was an adequate reaction to her point, I couldn't tell, but she did not say she disliked what I was suggesting. Nevertheless, she went on expressing her indignation at the Brussels bureaucracy and the creeping federalization of Europe which, she insisted, Britain must resist. She was no longer haranguing, but there was anger in her eyes. Britain was not like other European nations. Britain had won the war. We intended to remain a nation-state, she said, and so on. I had no choice but to say my bit, but I did so with a minimum of words and hoping to cause least offence in the light of her helpful attitude to my Bosnian committee.

'I am firmly in the pro-European camp,' I said, 'and have been since the beginnings of the European movement. So I would beg to differ.'

'I know, I know,' she replied with a reproachful look in her eyes.

'But even though I cannot agree with you,' I continued, 'I respect your views and I know why you are holding them.'

'Oh, well, well,' she said, in a grudging but good-natured tone, as though she was trying to tell me: now that's very generous of you, George, very generous ...

We left it at that.

CHAPTER 13

At a Stand-up Party

The wider political context in which my various meetings and contacts with Baroness Thatcher took place will be familiar to the contemporary newspaper reader. I have, therefore, deliberately avoided tiresome rehearsals of background and chronology. But I cannot spare the reader some indication of Margaret Thatcher's place in the British scheme of things as it is likely to appear to our successors.

They will certainly not find it easy to append a single label either to Margaret Thatcher's thinking or to her character. She was both conservative and rebellious; both an iconoclast and an admirer of authority and entitlement; an enemy of privilege as much as an upholder of the established order; both a savage critic of modern Britain and a determined keeper of its traditions. Her conservatism was accidental and exogenous – she was not destined to become a British Conservative. By temperament and ideology, she would have been a better fit in almost any country other than Britain. Yet, it was her 'otherness' at a time of prolonged British decline that fuelled her meteoric rise. In it, too, lies the clue to the gradual dissipation of her title to leadership in the eyes of the British people.

My journal ends on a note showing Margaret Thatcher in a mood of fretting and brewing rather than of cathartic reflection, as we would expect after so dramatic a career. It may well be that the purifying final act of her story is yet to be written.

Diary

8 March 1994

Noel Malcolm's outstanding history of Bosnia[1] was launched yesterday at a publisher's party in the offices of the Alliance to Defend

---

1. *Bosnia, a Short History*, London, 1994.

Bosnia-Herzegovina. Margaret Thatcher and Dennis Thatcher were there, and so among the notables was Michael Foot, an old Yugoslav hand, and a good selection of other Balkan 'experts'. The venue was distinctly scruffy, with a badly lit staircase leading up to the Alliance's rooms on the fourth floor. The lift was out of order. Dickens would have felt at home.

Noel and his book deserve better, but publishing in this country has always been a shoestring affair, and even when the publisher's purse (in this case Macmillan's) would permit a more respectable send-off, it is English chic to demonstrate a Spartan exterior if not downright poverty. Not the sort of thing I like. When some of my own books were launched at Brown's Hotel and the Westbury in the 1970s and 1980s, my good friend Maurice Temple-Smith accepted without demur that all the bills should be settled by Radio Free Europe.

But the quality of Noel's book, and the conversations surrounding it in the two small rooms we had filled to capacity, made up for the poor environment. Once again, Lady Thatcher was the centre of attention, but because she was being mobbed by people curious to catch a glimpse of her and hear her views, I made no attempt to join her. As the throng began to thin out, however, she saw me talking to some Macedonians in a corner and waved me over with a smile. She was debating with Daniel Johnson of *The Times* and Drago Stambuk, the Croatian chargé with whom the Centre for Policy Studies and I had closely cooperated when his country was being savaged by the Serbs.

MT treated me with considerable familiarity, touching me on the arm and thrusting her finger periodically at my chest to give weight to some point or other. Among the young blood standing around her, I was indeed an old friend in every sense of the word. Noel, ever modest, was holding back.

What did I make of the situation in Russia? she asked.

I said I could sense another implosion approaching.

What's an 'implosion'? she wanted to know with some irritation. I tried to explain.

The group began to fall silent, expecting, as I thought, to witness a punchy argument between MT, who was on wonderfully cantankerous form, and a supporter who could probably afford to go beyond expressing admiration and uttering platitudes.

Always loath to spoil other people's fun, I thought I'd keep to the festive spirit of the occasion, mixing a little irony into the banter I felt was coming.

'Aren't you too pessimistic?' MT challenged me. 'Why are you so pessimistic?'

I said it was not a question of optimism or pessimism but one of reading the facts. There was the semi-comical figure of Vladimir Zhirinovsky[1] on the Right, together with other, less comical and less conspicuous but none the less influential Rightists attracting a large following. On the Left, the old party cadres were still in office; the military were unrepentant, feeling they had been stabbed in the back. The three could form a common front against Yeltsin, sinking the reforms and frightening the wits out of Central and Eastern Europe.

MT felt I was overrating Zhirinovsky. I said perhaps I was, but the temptation to overrate him was great because he had such a fine talent for making outrageous and headline-catching statements. On a dull day, the Western press loved the wild Russian's antics. With all that, however, my impression was that Zhirinovsky responds to popular feeling all over Russia and needs to be watched.

'I'm not too worried about either the Right or the Left opposing Yeltsin's authority,' MT said. 'The danger arises if and when the two combine in a common front.'

I said this was already happening in certain areas and might go further in the future. Luckily, the splits within both were serious and would make it difficult to maintain a common front beyond a narrow band of issues and beyond a limited period of time. Yet, I said, the amnesty given to the October plotters was one worrying

---

1. Member of the Duma; ultra-nationalist chairman of the Liberal Democratic Party.

sign of the joint power of the neo-fascists and neo- (or, indeed, the old) communists.

MT agreed and showed great apprehension. How could an elected Duma subvert the rule of law by releasing a bunch of plotters under indictment for high treason? There should be some UN sanction against any such thing happening, she went on.

But what caused the real controversy between us was an airy remark I threw out half in jest half in earnest about the Russian people's traditional indiscipline and inclination to anarchy. What the 'dark masses' need, I said, is the periodic application of the whip, as so many Russians have been telling us. The present chaos, too, is waiting to be sorted out by a strong man of one kind or another.

To my surprise, MT took my mention of the whip literally and reacted with anger. 'How can you say such a thing, George?! No people should be ruled by the whip, no people at all. I've been to Russia and I found the people kind, sensitive and most hospitable. How can you talk about the whip?!' MT was deadly serious. Perhaps I should not have played on her sense of humour.

'Well,' I said, 'this is not my personal view but one that stares us in the face from the pages of Russian literature. Even today, many Russians will volunteer the opinion that only a Tsar-like figure can keep them in order. Stalin was aware of that and kept an orderly house; but look at what happened under the liberal Gorbachev. In 1985,' I went on, 'I predicted in the *Wall Street Journal* that Gorbachev might end up installing democracy using the methods of Stalin ...'

Again, my irony misfired. 'But not the whip, George,' MT repeated, 'No people need the whip. There is reason, there is persuasion. A strong government, yes, respect for authority, yes, but not the whip. I *am* surprised!'

The lighter touch having failed, I now decided to respond to Lady Thatcher's seriousness with seriousness.

'With respect,' I said, 'the Russian people's periodic ungovernability is proverbial and well documented in history. You yourself experienced ungovernability, although of the British kind, at the time of the miners' strike, and even that did not pass off without violence. So please try to transpose those relatively mild British reactions to a country in which serfdom was an accepted feature of life until 1861, and corporal punishment was commonplace. Then you will sense why the knout as a symbol of discipline is no outlandish symbol in Russian life. Personally, I abhor it as much as any man, but I'm trying to describe facts; I'm not passing judgement.'

This released another torrent of words I did not care to interrupt. There was a strange glitter in MT's eyes. She was tense, almost manic; her mind seemed centred on the next item in her stream of consciousness.

Finally I interjected. 'Some time ago,' I said, 'I sent you a volume of Custine[1] as background reading to the Soviet/Russian mentality. Wouldn't you agree that what I have been saying is in line with Custine's travelogue?'

'Yes, I've read it,' she answered, 'but Custine wrote about Russian conditions 150 years ago. You can't take that for your guide. Conditions change; people change.'

I wondered whether she would care to apply that principle to the German people and German character, remembering the views she had expressed at our 1990 Chequers seminar; but I kept my thoughts to myself.

MT then told us that she had also read Dostoevsky and Koestler and found that *Darkness at Noon* came directly out of *The Possessed*. I made no comment; it seemed useless to argue. MT was by now in love with her own voice and would not stop to listen.

'Koestler in that book speaks from his own experience; that is why his story is so formidably convincing,' she observed.

I tried to make the point, though without much hope of success, that Koestler had never been through a Soviet interrogation, but his imagination, his communist past and what he had read put him uncannily in phase with Soviet ways of thinking. But I was smothered by the lady's words. I explained as best I could that I had

---

1. The Marquis de Custine, *Journey for our Time*, 1839.

known Koestler well and had even discussed this very point with him in the 1960s and published the results;[1] but it was an exercise in futility. The lecturing went on.

'Why on earth are you so pessimistic, George?' she repeated with animation. 'Can't you see that we must speak the truth again and again because people have short memories, they don't read books and don't reflect? You and I are at the end of our lives; we have a duty to show the way to the young; we must pass on what we have thought and experienced.'

'Yes,' I said, 'on that point I very much agree with you,' and went on, perhaps a little pompously, to quote something from Goethe to reinforce her point: everything worth saying has already been said; our job is to say it again and say it better. I'm not sure, however, whether she took it in. Her mind was concentrated on herself.

'Do you realize', she said, 'that most of my supporters and admirers are young people? Isn't that remarkable?' I said it was remarkable; in me, however, I added, she had an admirer not quite so young.

Suddenly she switched back to communism.

'Is the Cold War returning?'

I said it would be far too early to say that it was, but there were signs of a revival of Russian national imperialism, driven forward by more or less the same people as had run the Soviet empire. We should remain on our guard. At this point Dennis hove into sight. He stood for a while behind his wife, 'I want to go,' he said.

MT turned round: 'I'm staying, dear, but *you* go.'

But Dennis, looking rather crestfallen, repeated 'I want to go,' at which point MT called one of her security men and told him to have Dennis driven home.

She then turned to nations and states. No one, she claimed, had yet presented a cogent theory of how nations and states relate to one another. What did I think?

---

1. Arthur Koestler, 'A Conversation', in G. R. Urban, *Talking to Eastern Europe*, London, 1964, pp. 97–117.

This was, of course, far too large a question to be threshed out at a stand-up party with drinks in hand. I tried to say that both Elie Kedourie and Hugh Seton-Watson had written important books on that very topic and both had advised her on various occasions – at times in my own presence. But I don't think she was listening; she was listening to herself. We were back on Bosnia.

'Self-determination is a principle wholly malign for the peace of the world,' she said. 'States just cannot be made to coincide with nations.'

I said: whatever we may feel about the rights and wrongs of national self-determination, it is there, in Principle VIII of the Helsinki Final Act, and has contributed to the disintegration of the Soviet empire. To that extent it has been of great practical value. But MT waved this aside.

'It is Woodrow Wilson, of course, who is ultimately responsible for the damaging myth of the single-nation state. Such states cannot work. Wilson got it all wrong. He is the one to be put in the dock of history.'

Our conversation was going nowhere. People had begun to leave. I removed myself gently from her circle.

Index